LEAPS:
FOR A MARKET-BASED DLOM

RONALD M. SEAMAN, FASA

AuthorHouse™
1663 Liberty Drive
Bloomington, IN 47403
www.authorhouse.com
Phone: 1-800-839-8640

First published by AuthorHouse 12/29/2011

ISBN: 978-1-4685-0004-2 (e)
ISBN: 978-1-4685-0005-9 (sc)

Library of Congress Control Number: 2011960270

Printed in the United States of America

This book is printed on acid-free paper.

TABLE OF CONTENTS

FOREWORD

I have three purposes in writing this book. One is to incorporate LEAPS knowledge and practice in one place. In the past I have published the annual studies and most of the other studies individually. This book puts it all together. Second, it presents the 2010 study, the fourth such study of all LEAPS. It compares the results of the studies and suggests some conclusions on how business appraisers should and should not use them. Finally, it offers my thoughts on what the discount for lack of marketability is and where the discussions of how to determine one are heading.

Where to place the numerous charts in a treatise like this is always an issue. I have chosen to place each chart as close as possible physically to the written discussion of its content, rather than in a group in the back.

If you have any comments or questions on my thoughts about LEAPS, feel free to call or write to me. Contact numbers are in my c.v. on the last pages of this text.

What is a DLOM?

There are numerous definitions of discount for lack of marketability (DLOM), some described by valuation scholars and some by various courts. All of them start with an illiquid business ownership interest, either controlling or non-controlling. In this book, I consider only non-controlling interests because LEAPS, by definition, are non-controlling interests.

All of the many definitions of the DLOM have four components in common:
   a.) the <u>ability</u> to convert the interest into cash;
   b.) the <u>time</u> necessary to convert the interest into cash;
   c.) the <u>cost</u> or expense to do so; and,
   d.) the <u>price at conversion</u>.
The discount for lack of marketability is a percentage reduction in the value of an illiquid business ownership interest necessary to compensate for these four components as compared to the marketability of a publicly traded stock.

Looking at the four components of marketability individually, the ability to convert the interest into cash means the legal ability; that is, am I as a stakeholder legally restricted from transferring my interest by a partnership agreement, a shareholder agreement, or any other legal impediment? This question is one of the "facts and circumstances" of each appraisal assignment. The time and the cost necessary to convert the interest into cash assume a decision to sell has been made and refer to the transaction period after that decision. Various practitioners have analyzed and written about these two components and how they can be measured. The fourth component, the price at conversion, also assumes that a decision to sell has been made. Implicit in the price at conversion is the concept of holding period – how long is the stakeholder likely to own the interest. In some cases, the likely holding period can be estimated fairly closely (for example, the ending date of the partnership). In many cases, the holding period can only be a reasoned guess.

Our studies of LEAPS have no relevance to component #1, the ability to convert an interest to cash. In the evaluation of the cost and the time to convert an interest to cash, LEAPS provide a known baseline. LEAPS are small minority interests and can be sold as quickly as public shares and for about the same cost. LEAPS also provide a known baseline holding period because they are issued in October and November of each year and expire in mid-January either two or three years later; that is, a maximum life span of about 14 months or 26 months.

In recent years some appraisers have begun to separate the DLOM into two parts: marketability and liquidity. By "marketability" they mean the "ability" component, defined as the legal ability to sell the interest. All three other components are usually included in the term "liquidity." In this book, I avoid definitional issues by using the term "discount for lack of marketability" predominantly. I believe that thinking of the discount in terms of the four components described above adds clarity to the issues. Those components clearly are embodied in the well-known "Mandelbaum factors" described in that U.S. Tax Court case.[1] In addition, considering the four components separately suggests a direction for future research on the discount for lack of marketability.

However defined, the discount for lack of marketability usually is, as we all know, a significant reduction in the value of an interest. For that reason, the courts are requiring appraisers to support and substantiate in more detail their conclusions of an "appropriate" discount.

LEAPS provide market evidence of the "price at conversion" component of the DLOM. That portion of the discount is often the largest portion of the total discount because of the price risk involved in any lengthy holding period. In defining the discount, writers describe the "the price at conversion" portion of the discount for lack of liquidity as at "a known price"[2] or as "realizing the expected amount of the net proceeds."[3] As described later in more detail, LEAPS are publicly traded, long-term put options that can be purchased at the same price an investor would pay for a share of common stock at the same time. The put option provides the investor the ability to sell the underlying stock in the future for the same price she/he paid for it. Therefore, it provides the investor insurance against loss during the holding period, or what we call "price protection." And, it provides that price protection at a known cost – the cost of the put option. The cost of the put option as a percentage of the price of the underlying stock is the cost of price protection as defined

1   Bernard Mandelbaum et al. v. Commissioner, T.C. Memo 1995-255 (June 12, 1995).

2   Glazer, Russell T., "Understanding the Valuation Discount for Lack of Marketability," The CPA Journal, N. Y. State Society of CPAs, August 2005.

3   Pratt, Shannon P., Valuing A Business, The Analysis and Appraisal of Closely Held Companies, 5th Edition, p. 417.

in a public market. It is the cost of insurance that provides the "known price" or "expected amount of the net proceeds" in the definition of DLOM. In this paper, we use the words "cost of price protection" and "discount" interchangeably and, in this context, synonymously.

The reasoning for the use of LEAPS is not original with me. In September 2003 Robert R. Trout, PhD, CFA published an article in Business Valuation Review titled "Minimum Marketability Discounts." Trout wrote, "The reason a marketability discount exists at all is because a buyer of a security that lacks marketability…is subject to a potential loss of equity value during the time period when the stock cannot be sold…considering the insurance characteristics of puts provides some information as to the minimum discount necessary for buyers to purchase stock…that is unmarketable." [4] The studies I have done since 2005 simply build on Trout's thesis.

---

4   Trout, Robert R., "Minimum Marketability Discounts," Business Valuation Review, September 2003, p.124.

What Are LEAPS?

Long-Term Equity Anticipation Securities (LEAPS) are exchange listed options that grant "the buyer (holder) the right, but not the obligation, to buy, in the case of a call, or to sell, in the case of a put, a specified amount of the underlying asset at a predetermined price on or before a given date."[5] During the option term, which ranges from 6 to 26 months, LEAPS are a form of insurance against price fluctuations in publicly-traded stocks.

LEAPS are listed on several stock exchanges and are actively traded. They are American-style options that may be exercised at any time prior to the expiration date. LEAPS are issued in September, October and November each year and expire on the third Saturday of January either two or three years later.

As an example, let's assume you purchased 100 shares of Proctor and Gamble stock at a certain price, say $50.00 per share, in November 2010. At the same time, you could have purchased a LEAPS put option

---

5   The Options Clearing Corporation, www.optionsclearing.com/publications/
     leaps/intro.jsp.

on that stock that expires in January 2012 (approximately 14 months to its expiration) or a longer term option that expires in January 2013 (approximately 26 months to expiration). The longer term put option would allow you to sell that P & G stock at $50.00 per share at any time until January 19, 2013; thus guaranteeing that you would not lose money. The cost to you of that put option would be a known price, say $7.10 per share, or 14.2% ($7.10 ÷ $50.00). That $7.10 would have been your cost of price protection for the 26 months until the option expires. The cost of a LEAPS put option "provide(s) a medium to long-term insurance or hedge for stock owners in the event of a substantial decline in their stock."[6] The cost of eliminating the risk of loss in value during the holding period – "the cost of price protection" - clearly is a significant component of the discount for lack of marketability (DLOM).

---

6   Chicago Board of Exchange, www.cboe.com/LearnCenter/FaqLEAPS.aspx

LEAPS Studies

Purposes Of The Studies

Our objective in studying LEAPS is to contribute to improved substantiation of the discount for lack of marketability, which has long been a concern of both valuation practitioners and courts. The data collected in the studies enables us to determine how discounts vary by time, size of company, volatility or risk of the company, profitability and other factors. The data also suggests which financial attributes (i.e., size, debt, dividends, etc.) affect the size of the DLOM and to what extent. The analysis of the costs of LEAPS with different times to expiration provides some insight into the effect of holding period on discounts for lack of marketability. The following chart shows the overall results for all companies in our four studies:

Costs of Price Protection: Annual Comparisons

Date of Survey Data	Aug. 2006	Nov. 2008	Nov. 2009	Dec. 2010
Months To Expiration	30	26	26	25 1/2
	2009 Option	2011 Option	2012 Option	2013 Option
No. of companies	897	623	577	650
Mean	20.5%	43.2%	27.9%	25.9%
Median	17.4%	40.6%	26.1%	23.0%
25% percentile	13.4%	34.0%	21.8%	19.7%
75% percentile	23.9%	49.2%	31.8%	28.4%

2010 LEAPS STUDY

The latest study is of the costs of LEAPS put options in early December 2010. Earlier years' studies are available in their entirety at the website www.dlom-info.com. In December 2010 LEAPS were available on about 795 operating companies. From this group, we excluded LEAPS of a few foreign companies for which no financial information was available and LEAPS of companies whose stock price was less than $2.50 per share, the lowest cost of a LEAPS put option. Remaining were 774 operating companies with 2012 LEAPS (13 ½ -month duration) and 650 companies with 2013 LEAPS (25 ½ -month duration). For some companies there were 2012 LEAPS and not 2013 LEAPS. A larger percentage of smaller companies (than larger companies) did not have the longer term LEAPS; that is, the smaller the company, the less likely it was to have the 2013 LEAPS.

The elements of the DLOM explored in this study are:
  a) discounts by size of a company's total revenues;

b) discounts by size of a company's total assets;

c) discounts by a company's beta;

d) discounts by profit margin (% of net income after taxes to revenues);

e) discounts by return on equity (% of net income after taxes to shareholders' equity);

f) discounts by debt/equity ratio (the ratio of total debt to shareholders' equity);

g) discounts by industry.

For all companies, we obtained the following information:

Data	Source
LEAPS Put Option "Asked" Price	Chicago Board of Exchange, Delayed Market Quotes www.cboe.com./DelayedQuoteTable.aspx
Underlying Stock Price	(Same source as for option price.)
Net Revenues (latest full year)[7]	Usually from Yahoo! Finance. When not readily available there, from the SEC's Edgar website.[8]
Total Assets (latest year end)	(Same source as for Revenues.)
Total Liabilities (latest year end)	(Same source as for Revenues.) Defined as long-term, short-term and current liabilities.

---

7   In most cases, the latest full year reported ended December 31, 2009.

8   For financial institutions (primarily banks), total revenues were calculated as interest income (before expenses) plus non-interest income.

Shareholders' Equity (latest year end)	(Same source as for Revenues.) Defined as "equity available to common shareholders."
Net Income (latest year end)	(Same source as for Revenues.) Defined as "net income available to common shareholders."
Beta (latest available date)	Yahoo! Finance
Industry	As defined in Yahoo! Finance. Consists of 9 major industry "Sectors" and 235 sub-categories.

DISCOUNT CALCULATIONS

The percentage costs of the put options were calculated as the cost of the option divided by the stock price. Because long-term options are usually sold in (cost) increments of $2.50 or $5.00, very few stock prices are precisely equivalent. For example, on December 2, 2010, Minnesota Mining and Manufacturing (MMM) stock sold for $86.94 per share. One could buy a 2013 LEAPS put option at $85.00 for $12.50 per share, or a $90.00 option at $15.15 per share. We calculate a hypothetical option cost to match the $86.94 stock price exactly, using what we call a "Distance Weighted Option Cost." Simply, it is the same proportion of the increased option cost as the relationship between the actual stock price and the next higher and lower option prices.

For example, using the MMM prices on December 2, we calculated the cost of a put option for $86.94 as a straight-line percentage increase in the actual option cost difference between $85.00 and $90.00. Thus, the stock price, $86.94, is $1.94 above the $85.00 strike price, or 38.8% of the $5.00 difference in strike prices ($1.94 ÷ $5.00). The difference in put option costs is $2.65 ($15.15 - $12.50). So we add 38.8% of the difference ($2.65 x .388 = $1.03) to the lower option cost ($12.50) to arrive at a "Distance Weighted Option Cost" of $13.53. Dividing that number by the stock price results in a percentage cost of 15.6% ($13.53 ÷ $86.94).

Expressed in a formula, the calculation is:

Step 1   Share Price – Strike 1 Option Price

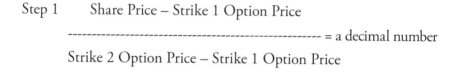

-- = a decimal number

Strike 2 Option Price – Strike 1 Option Price

Step 2   (Option 2 Cost – Option 1 Cost) x decimal number from Step 1
+ Option 1 Cost = new put option cost

Step 3   The new put option cost divided by the share price is the cost of price protection (expressed as a percentage).

LEAPS Studies: Financial Characteristics

Much financial data is available on publicly traded companies. One purpose of our studies of LEAPS is to assess which financial attributes affect the costs of price protection or discounts and to what extent they affect them. The conclusions are that the more important influences on discounts are company size, in revenues and assets, and beta or company specific risk. The measures of dividend yield, profitability, return on equity and debt/equity ratio are somewhat less important unless at the extremes, such as very high dividends or significant losses or very high debt. The supporting data for those conclusions follows.

Cost of Price Protection By Revenue Size: 2010 Study

As in prior years, the 2010 Study presents company revenues in three basic size categories and two smaller breakdowns. The three basic sizes are companies with over $10 billion dollars of revenues, those with $1 billion to $10 billion in revenues, and those with under $1 billion dollars of revenues. Because appraisers of privately held companies frequently value smaller companies, the under $1 billion revenue category is further broken down into companies with less than $500 million of revenues and those with under $100 million. (See Chart I.)

Within each size category, and within each measure (mean, median, percentiles), the costs/discounts increase as revenue size decreases. Thus, it is clear that company size is an important determinant of the DLOM. For companies with revenues under $500 million, the median cost of price protection for the 25 ½-month holding period is 35%, and the range of the middle 50% of costs is from 28% to 46.6%. Because the average cost is higher than the median, we know that actual results are skewed toward higher discounts. Even for companies with less than $1 billion of revenues, costs of price protection and discounts are significant, from 26% to 41% with a median of 31%.

In Chart I, the column headed "Incr.* '13>'12" shows the absolute percentage increase in the discount for an additional 12 months' time; that is, the time to expiration of the nearer term discount, 13 1/2

Chart I
Costs of Price Protection By Revenue Size: 2010

Months To Expiration of Option	13 1/2	25 1/2	
	2012	2013	Incr.*
Revenues: All Companies	Option	Option	'13-'12
Count	774	650	
Average	18.5%	25.9%	7.3%
Median	16.8%	23.0%	6.2%
25th Percentile	14.2%	19.7%	5.5%
75th Percentile	20.9%	28.4%	7.5%
Revenues: $10 Billion or More			
Count	228	214	
Average	14.6%	20.6%	6.0%
Median	14.0%	19.9%	5.9%
25th Percentile	12.5%	18.2%	5.7%
75th Percentile	16.2%	22.4%	6.2%
Revenues: $1 Billion to $10 Billion			
Count	360	300	
Average	17.4%	24.6%	7.2%
Median	16.8%	23.4%	6.7%
25th Percentile	14.6%	20.7%	6.0%
75th Percentile	19.3%	27.2%	7.9%
Revenues: Under $1 Billion			
Count	186	136	
Average	25.6%	36.9%	11.3%
Median	22.7%	31.1%	8.5%
25th Percentile	19.0%	25.8%	6.8%
75th Percentile	27.9%	41.3%	13.5%
Revenues: Under $500 Million			
Count	118	83	
Average	28.2%	40.5%	12.3%
Median	25.2%	35.0%	9.7%
25th Percentile	21.1%	28.1%	7.0%
75th Percentile	32.5%	46.6%	14.2%
Revenues: Under $100 M			
Count	42	31	
Average	36.4%	54.9%	18.5%
Median	34.4%	50.4%	16.0%
25th Percentile	27.6%	36.9%	9.3%
75th Percentile	44.0%	64.3%	20.3%

Survey data from early December 2010.

* "Incr. '13>'12" is the absolute percentage increase in the discount for an additional
   12 months of time; that is, the time from the shorter term discount, 13 1/2 months for
   the shorter term 2012 option, to 25 1/2 months for the 2013 option.

months for a 2012 option, to 25 1/2 months for the 2013 option. It demonstrates the magnitude of the increased cost of the additional year of price protection. For example, in Chart I we can see that the "Increase" becomes greater as company size becomes smaller; a median of 5.9% for companies with over $10 billion revenues; versus 6.7% for companies with $1 billion to $10 billion; 8.5% for companies with under $1 billion; and 9.7% for companies with under $500 million. Clearly, the market recognizes that both smaller size and a longer holding period increase investor risk.[9]

It is instructive to look at the range of the middle 50% of companies in Chart I to see how that range increases as revenue size decreases. The following chart is extracted from Chart I. The "Breadth of the Range of the Middle 50% of Discounts" is arrived at simply by subtracting the 25th percentile from the 75th percentile in each revenue size. One implication of this chart for appraisers is that, if I am appraising a company with over $10 billion in revenues, I can be quite confident using a minimum DLOM of 19.9%, the median result at this time, because the range of the middle 50% is small. However, for a subject company with smaller total revenue my rationale for choosing a particular discount will have to be much more specific because the "breadth" is wide. That fact is more evident with a holding period of 25 ½ months or longer as the breadth of the middle 50% is even wider.

---

9   It is interesting to note that, in the charts comparing one or more years, the numbers in the "Incr.* 'yr>'yr", are frequently larger for the longer term option (i.e., the 2013 option) in December 2010 than for the comparable option in 2009. This suggests that the market sees greater uncertainty of the future in December 2010 than it did in December 2009. The same fact appears in analyses of total assets, beta, returns on equity, etc.

Breadth of the Range of the Middle 50% of Discounts

	2012 Option	2013 Option
Months to expiration of option:	13 1/2	25 1/2
Revenues: $10 Billion or More	3.7%	4.2%
Revenues: $1 Billion to $10 Billion	4.7%	6.5%
Revenues: Under $1 Billion	8.9%	15.5%
Revenues: Under $500 Million	11.4%	18.5%
Revenues: Under $100 Million	16.4%	27.4%

COST OF PRICE PROTECTION BY REVENUE SIZE: ANNUAL COMPARISONS

Chart II shows the costs of price protection by revenue size in each of our four studies - from data collected in August 2006 to data collected in early December 2010. Obviously, economic conditions varied dramatically during that period, and the affects are interesting to see on the costs of price protection and on discounts. In general, discounts in November 2008 were double or triple those in August 2006. In late 2009 and 2010 discounts shrank but are still significantly higher than in 2006. These studies illustrate that discounts for lack of marketability change over time and are not static. Other studies show that discounts change rapidly. [10]

All four studies show the same, very clear pattern: that discounts increase as revenue size decreases. In addition, all studies show that the costs of price protection for companies with less than $500 million in revenues

---

10 The speed with which discounts change is illustrated further in a 2010 study of 10 selected stocks. The study is entitled "How Fast Do DLOMs Change?" and is included in a later chapter of this book.

will often be in the range of 30% to 50%. In 2010, even companies with revenues over $10 billion commonly will have discounts in the neighborhood of 20%. On the other hand, the fact that significant changes in discounts do occur in the market suggests that a valuation practitioner must base a discount for lack of marketability on data that is current with his valuation date.

It is interesting to observe the changes from year to year in the cost of an additional 12 months of price protection (the columns headed "Incr.* Yr. > Yr."). All of those costs increased dramatically in 2008 from 2006, declined in 2009, and increased again in 2010. At no time were the costs of the additional 12 months as low as in 2006.

Chart II
Costs of Price Protection By Revenue Size: Annual Comparisons

Date of Survey Data Months To Expiration	August 2006 30		November 2008 26		November 2009 26		December 2010 25 1/2	
	2009 Option	Incr.* '09 > '08	2011 Option	Incr.* '11 > '10	2012 Option	Incr.* '12 >'11	2013 Option	Incr.* 13 >'12
All companies								
No. of companies	897		623		577		650	
Mean	20.5%	4.2%	43.2%	6.9%	27.9%	6.2%	25.9%	7.3%
Median	17.4%	3.5%	40.6%	7.2%	26.1%	5.8%	23.0%	6.2%
25% percentile	13.4%	2.9%	34.0%	6.5%	21.8%	4.9%	19.7%	5.5%
75% percentile	23.9%	4.7%	49.2%	7.5%	31.8%	7.2%	28.4%	7.5%
Revenues of $10 Billion or Greater								
No. of companies	231		216		218		214	
Mean	14.6%	3.1%	37.1%	6.3%	23.8%	5.6%	20.6%	6.0%
Median	13.4%	2.9%	35.0%	6.6%	22.8%	5.6%	19.9%	5.9%
25% percentile	11.3%	2.5%	29.0%	5.5%	19.8%	5.2%	18.2%	5.7%
75% percentile	16.3%	3.5%	42.9%	6.7%	26.6%	5.9%	22.4%	6.2%
Revenues of $1 Billion to $10 Billion								
No. of companies	407		281		274		300	
Mean	18.5%	3.7%	43.9%	8.2%	28.6%	6.5%	24.6%	7.2%
Median	16.6%	3.0%	41.4%	7.8%	28.0%	6.9%	23.4%	6.7%
25% percentile	13.6%	2.9%	35.8%	7.4%	23.3%	5.4%	20.7%	6.0%
75% percentile	21.3%	4.2%	50.1%	9.7%	32.5%	7.8%	27.2%	7.9%
Revenues Under $1 Billion								
No. of companies	259		126		85		136	
Mean	29.0%	5.8%	52.3%	10.4%	35.8%	8.8%	36.9%	11.3%
Median	25.9%	5.4%	47.9%	9.9%	32.3%	7.0%	31.1%	8.5%
25% percentile	20.3%	4.2%	39.3%	7.6%	27.7%	6.9%	25.8%	6.8%
75% percentile	33.5%	6.7%	62.3%	13.7%	38.1%	7.6%	41.3%	13.5%
Revenues Under $500 million								
No. of companies	171		79		52		83	
Mean	31.2%	5.5%	53.7%	11.2%	38.9%	10.3%	40.5%	12.3%
Median	28.6%	5.9%	50.1%	10.5%	34.5%	8.6%	35.0%	9.7%
25% percentile	22.8%	4.3%	40.8%	8.6%	28.9%	7.5%	28.1%	7.0%
75% percentile	35.9%	7.1%	61.5%	12.4%	41.8%	9.2%	46.6%	14.2%
Revenues Under $100 million								
No. of companies	65		24		17		31	
Mean	38.1%	6.7%	64.6%	13.9%	50.4%	13.5%	54.9%	18.5%
Median	35.0%	7.7%	61.5%	14.3%	47.6%	12.1%	50.4%	16.0%
25% percentile	28.3%	5.7%	51.6%	13.6%	34.4%	5.2%	36.9%	9.3%
75% percentile	44.4%	7.5%	70.8%	8.4%	56.8%	15.0%	64.3%	20.3%

* "Increase" is the absolute percentage increase in the discount for an additional 12 months of time; that is, the time from the shorter term discount, 13 1/2 months for a 2012 option, to 25 1/2 months for the 2013 option.

Cost of Price Protection By Total Assets Size: 2010 Study

The 2010 Study (Chart III) again shows a strong correlation between total asset size and discounts: as size of assets decreases, discount increases. Median cost of price protection for a period of 25 ½ months for a company with total assets over $10 billion is 20.3%. For companies with less than $500 million in total assets, the median cost or discount more than doubles, to 43.1%. As with the prior analysis by revenue size, it is clear with total assets that the range of the middle 50% of discounts broadens as size decreases. For example, for the longer term option (2013) and for companies with over $10 billion in total assets, the range of the middle 50% of companies is 4.4%, that is, discounts of from 18.5% to 22.9%. For the next smallest size category, companies with total assets of from $1 billion to $10 billion, the range of the middle 50% of companies is 7.7%. For companies with total assets under $1 billion, the range is 18.9%, and for companies with under $500 million in total assets the range is 24.6%.

Chart III
Costs of Price Protection By Total Assets Size: 2010

Months To Expiration of Option	13 1/2	25 1/2	
	2012 Option	2013 Option	Incr.* '13-'12
Total Assets: All Companies			
Count	772	649	
Average	19.0%	26.5%	7.6%
Median	16.8%	23.0%	6.2%
25th Percentile	14.2%	19.7%	5.5%
75th Percentile	20.9%	28.3%	7.5%
Total Assets: $10 Billion or More			
Count	302	284	
Average	15.2%	21.5%	6.3%
Median	14.5%	20.3%	5.8%
25th Percentile	12.9%	18.5%	5.6%
75th Percentile	16.5%	22.9%	6.4%
Total Assets: $1 Billion to $10 Billion			
Count	350	282	
Average	18.1%	26.1%	8.0%
Median	17.3%	24.5%	7.2%
25th Percentile	15.2%	21.5%	6.2%
75th Percentile	20.7%	29.2%	8.5%
Total Assets: Under $1 Billion			
Count	120	83	
Average	28.0%	39.9%	12.0%
Median	24.4%	33.4%	8.9%
25th Percentile	21.0%	27.8%	6.8%
75th Percentile	32.4%	46.7%	14.3%
Total Assets: Under $500 Million			
Count	64	43	
Average	33.3%	48.4%	15.1%
Median	31.4%	43.1%	11.6%
25th Percentile	24.7%	32.9%	8.2%
75th Percentile	41.3%	57.5%	16.2%

Survey data from early December 2010.

* "Incr. '13>'12" is the absolute percentage increase in the discount for an additional 12 months of time; that is, the time from the shorter term discount, 13 1/2 months for the shorter term 2012 option, to 25 1/2 months for the 2013 option.

Cost of Price Protection By Total Assets Size: Annual Comparisons

As with our analysis of revenue sizes, discounts uniformly increase in all years as asset sizes decrease. (See Chart IV.) The changes from year to year reflecting economic conditions are evident, again emphasizing the need for discount data that is current with the valuation date of the property being appraised.

The conclusions of the studies of costs of price protection by revenue size and by total asset size are very similar. And, the bases (revenue size and total asset size) measure essentially the same things about a company. Therefore, it is obvious that a practicing business valuator should not choose a discount based on revenue size and also add a discount based on asset size.

Chart IV
Costs of Price Protection By Total Assets Size: Annual Comparisons

Date of Survey Data Months To Expiration	August 2006 30		November 2008 26		November 2009 26		December 2010 25 1/2	
	2009 Option	Incr.* '09 > '08	2011 Option	Incr.* '11 > '10	2012 Option	Increase '12 >'11	2013 Option	Incr.* 13 >'12
All companies								
No. of companies	894		628		574		649	
Mean	20.5%	4.2%	43.4%	7.0%	27.9%	6.2%	26.5%	7.6%
Median	17.4%	3.5%	40.8%	7.3%	26.1%	5.8%	23.0%	6.2%
25% percentile	11.2%	2.3%	34.0%	6.5%	21.8%	4.9%	19.7%	5.5%
75% percentile	16.5%	3.1%	50.0%	8.3%	31.8%	7.2%	28.3%	7.5%
Total Assets of $10 Billion or Greater								
No. of companies	294		268		251		284	
Mean	14.5%	3.0%	38.7%	6.3%	24.7%	6.0%	21.5%	6.3%
Median	13.4%	2.9%	36.1%	6.3%	23.4%	5.6%	20.3%	5.8%
25% percentile	11.2%	2.4%	30.1%	5.9%	20.4%	5.5%	18.5%	5.6%
75% percentile	16.3%	3.1%	44.3%	6.5%	27.9%	6.8%	22.9%	6.4%
Total Assets of $1 Billion to $10 Billion								
No. of companies	407		276		257		282	
Mean	19.6%	3.8%	45.1%	8.7%	28.7%	6.4%	26.1%	8.0%
Median	17.7%	3.6%	42.2%	8.3%	27.8%	6.7%	24.5%	7.2%
25% percentile	14.8%	3.2%	36.3%	7.7%	23.3%	5.2%	21.5%	6.2%
75% percentile	22.1%	4.0%	51.4%	10.1%	32.4%	7.4%	29.2%	8.5%
Total Assets Under $1 Billion								
No. of companies	193		84		66		83	
Mean	31.6%	6.5%	52.5%	10.8%	37.0%	9.2%	39.9%	12.0%
Median	27.6%	5.4%	49.2%	11.4%	33.4%	7.7%	33.4%	8.9%
25% percentile	22.8%	4.9%	40.0%	8.1%	28.2%	7.0%	27.8%	6.8%
75% percentile	35.4%	7.3%	59.2%	10.7%	38.9%	6.5%	46.7%	14.3%
Total Assets Under $500 million								
No. of companies	111		47		31		43	
Mean	33.6%	5.6%	58.5%	12.8%	44.1%	11.6%	48.4%	15.1%
Median	30.4%	5.6%	54.5%	11.5%	37.6%	7.8%	43.1%	11.6%
25% percentile	25.2%	5.5%	45.9%	12.3%	33.8%	8.0%	32.9%	8.2%
75% percentile	38.5%	6.9%	68.9%	15.5%	48.6%	10.4%	57.5%	16.2%

* "Increase" is the absolute percentage increase in the discount for an additional 12 months of time; that is, the time from the shorter period discount, 14 months for a 2012 option to 26 months for the 2013 option.

Cost of Price Protection As A Function of Dividend Yield: 2010 Study

Literature on discounts for lack of marketability frequently suggests that dividend-paying stocks warrant lower discounts because investors in such stocks are getting some return during their (frequently long) holding periods. An analysis of LEAPS provides some facts on that issue.

Chart V shows the costs of price protection by dividend yields for all operating company LEAPS as of early December 2010. Beginning at the bottom of the Chart, we see that the costs of price protection of 2013 options on 351 dividend-paying stocks are uniformly (average, median and quartiles) lower than the costs of 364 non-dividend-paying stocks. In addition, costs of the additional 12 months of price protection (between the 2012 and 2013 options) are smaller for dividend-paying stocks than for non-dividend-paying stocks (the column headed "Incr. '13 > '12), and the range of discounts for the middle 50% of companies is smaller for dividend-paying stocks. Neither of these observations is very surprising as the universe of non-dividend paying companies is very diverse ranging from start-up technology or medical research companies to large established manufacturing companies like Toyota which paid no dividends in the study year.

Also in Chart V the breakdown of discounts by size of dividend yield shows little difference between stocks yielding more than 4% (of their market price) and those yielding less. In fact, the lowest discounts are for those companies yielding between 1% and 4%.

Chart V
Cost of Price Protection As A Function of Dividend Yield

	2012 Option	2013 Option	Incr. * '13 > '12
Dividend Yield of 4.0% or More			
Count	48	46	
Average	16.2%	25.4%	9.2%
Median	15.3%	23.0%	7.6%
25th Percentile	13.2%	19.4%	6.2%
75th Percentile	18.1%	27.4%	9.3%
Dividend Yield from 1.0% to 4.0%			
Count	205	183	
Average	14.7%	21.0%	6.2%
Median	14.5%	20.1%	5.6%
25th Percentile	12.4%	17.8%	5.3%
75th Percentile	16.3%	22.9%	6.6%
Dividend Yield Below 1.0%			
Count	137	122	
Average	16.3%	22.5%	6.2%
Median	15.9%	22.2%	6.3%
25th Percentile	14.6%	20.2%	5.5%
75th Percentile	17.5%	24.0%	6.5%
No Dividend Yield			
Count	468	364	
Average	21.2%	29.4%	8.2%
Median	19.1%	26.0%	6.9%
25th Percentile	15.3%	21.3%	6.0%
75th Percentile	24.6%	33.5%	8.9%
Dividend Yield (Any Size)			
Count	390	351	
Average	15.4%	22.1%	6.6%
Median	15.1%	21.1%	6.0%
25th Percentile	13.2%	19.0%	5.8%
75th Percentile	17.2%	24.0%	6.9%

* "Increase" is the absolute percentage increase in the discount for an additional 12 months of time; that is, the time from the shorter term discount, 13 1/2 months for a 2012 option, to 25 1/2 months for the 2013 option.

Cost of Price Protection As A Function of Dividend Yield: Annual Comparisons

Chart VI compares the costs of price protection by dividend yields at roughly the same times in 2009 and 2010.[11] As with other measures, discounts are lower in 2010 than 2009. The patterns or differences between yielding and non-yielding stocks are the same. It appears that there is a 4% to 5% lower (absolute) cost of price protection for dividend-paying stocks. The range of the middle 50% of discounts is greater in non-dividend-paying companies than in companies paying dividends. However, this is not surprising considering the large differences among non-dividend-payers in size and in life cycle. Again, stocks with dividend yields between 1% and 4% have lower discounts than either higher or lower yielding stocks.

---

11 A similar study was done with data from late 2008. The category breakdowns used were different so the results can not be compared, but the general conclusions about effects on discounts were similar.

Chart VI
Cost of Price Protection As A Function of Dividend Yield
(Longer term options)

Date of Survey Data	Nov. 2009	Dec. 2010
Months To Option Expiration	26	25 1/2

Dividend Yield of 4.0% or More

Count	43	46
Mean	26.4%	25.4%
Median	24.9%	23.0%
25% percentile	21.1%	19.4%
75% percentile	30.5%	27.4%

Dividend Yield of 1.0% to 4.0%

Count	210	183
Mean	24.6%	21.0%
Median	23.6%	20.1%
25% percentile	20.1%	17.8%
75% percentile	28.7%	22.9%

Dividend Yield Below 1.0%

Count	75	122
Mean	27.2%	22.5%
Median	25.8%	22.2%
25% percentile	21.9%	20.2%
75% percentile	30.5%	24.0%

No Dividend Yield

Count	249	364
Mean	31.0%	29.4%
Median	28.6%	26.0%
25% percentile	24.2%	21.3%
75% percentile	34.7%	33.5%

Dividend Yield (Any Size)

Count	328	351
Mean	25.4%	22.1%
Median	24.3%	21.1%
25th Percentile	20.9%	18.9%
75th Percentile	29.5%	24.0%

* "Increase" is the absolute percentage increase in the discount for an additional 12 months of time; that is, the time from the shorter term discount, 13 1/2 months for a 2012 option, to 25 1/2 months for the 2013 option.

We know from analyzing the costs of price protection based on company revenue size that discounts increase as company size decreases. That fact poses the question: are the differences in the cost of price protection due to dividend yields really a result of company size, not dividends; that is, are the differences in dividend yields a result of the fact that larger companies are more likely to pay dividends than smaller companies? The following analysis strongly suggests the latter interpretation: that the lower discounts are largely a function of company size, at least in the public markets for LEAPS.

Revenue Sizes of Companies Paying Dividends
(Data from December 2010)

All Companies Paying Dividends	$ in M's
Average Revenue Size	$21,489.3
Median Revenue Size	$8,111.3
25th Percentile Revenue Size	$3,184.0
75th Percentile Revenue Size	$22,832.0
Minimum Revenue Size	$0.0

All Companies Not Paying Dividends	
Average Revenue Size	$5,984.2
Median Revenue Size	$1,449.1
25th Percentile Revenue Size	$384.8
75th Percentile Revenue Size	$4,571.8
Maximum Revenue Size	$202,814.0

So what, if any, guidance does the study of dividend yields provide the typical business valuation practitioner? If the company being valued pays an annual dividend up to 5% or so, a modest reduction in the marketability discount may be warranted. Other than that the field of data is so wide that it does not provide much guidance.

Cost of Price Protection As A Function of A Company's Beta: 2010 Study

This study uses a company's beta as shown in Yahoo Finance. The beta is defined as "The measure of a fund's or a stock's risk in relation to the market…A beta of 1.5 means that a stock's excess return is expected to move 1.5 times the market excess returns." [12] "Excess return" is defined as "the difference between the asset return and the riskless rate." [13] The calculation of quintiles in Chart VII (and in other analyses) is based on 2012 options. Because some companies do not offer 2013 options, the 2013 counts will be less.

Chart VII shows that the cost of price protection becomes uniformly higher as betas get higher. The increases in discounts become more noticeable (greater) in betas above 1.1, and especially above 1.5. The costs of the second 12 months of price protection (the column headed "Incr. * '13>'12") show the same pattern; that is, the costs are roughly the same when company betas are below 1.47, but the costs increase with higher betas.

---

12 Yahoo Financial Glossary, http://biz.yahoo.com/f/g/bb.html.
13 Ibid.

Chart VII

Cost of Price Protection As A Function of A Company's Beta: 2010 Study

	2012 Option	2013 Option	Incr. * '13>'12
Beta: 1.95 and Higher (1st Quintile)			
Count	153	122	
Average	22.6%	33.9%	11.4%
Median	21.0%	29.8%	8.8%
25th Percentile	17.9%	24.7%	6.9%
75th Percentile	25.3%	36.1%	10.8%
Beta: 1.47 Through 1.94 (2nd Quintile)			
Count	153	126	
Average	19.9%	26.2%	6.3%
Median	17.4%	24.1%	6.7%
25th Percentile	15.9%	22.1%	6.2%
75th Percentile	20.9%	28.3%	7.4%
Beta: 1.11 Through 1.46 (3rd Quintile)			
Count	153	132	
Average	17.8%	24.7%	6.9%
Median	16.0%	22.0%	6.0%
25th Percentile	14.6%	20.1%	5.5%
75th Percentile	18.6%	25.7%	7.0%
Beta: 0.74 Through 1.10 (4th Quintile)			
Count	152	132	
Average	16.1%	22.6%	6.5%
Median	14.6%	20.7%	6.0%
25th Percentile	13.2%	18.4%	5.3%
75th Percentile	17.4%	25.0%	7.7%
Beta: Negative Through 0.74 (5th Quintile)			
Count	152	129	
Average	16.2%	22.0%	5.8%
Median	13.6%	19.4%	5.9%
25th Percentile	11.6%	17.0%	5.4%
75th Percentile	18.9%	23.4%	4.5%

* "Increase" is the absolute percentage increase in the discount for an additional 12 months of time; that is, the time from the shorter term discount, 13 1/2 months for a 2012 option, to 25 1/2 months for the 2013 option.

COST OF PRICE PROTECTION AS A FUNCTION OF A COMPANY'S BETA: ANNUAL COMPARISONS

Chart VIII shows the results of the latest three years' studies. As before, 2010 discounts have come down 30% to 45% from 2008 highs. Costs of an additional 12 months of price protection have also decreased but not by the same magnitude. Historically, the trend is the same: that the cost of price protection/the discount decreases as a company's beta decreases.

Chart VIII
Cost of Price Protection By A Company's Beta: Annual Comparisons

Date of Survey Data Months To Option Expiration	November 2008 26		November 2009 26		December 2010 25 1/2	
	2011 Option	Incr. * '11 > '10	2012 Option	Incr. * '12 >'11	2013 Option	Incr. * 13 >'12
Beta: 1.83/1.99 and Higher (1st Quintile)						
No. of companies	119		107		122	
Mean	51.2%	7.9%	35.0%	7.0%	33.9%	11.4%
Median	47.2%	7.7%	33.0%	7.0%	29.8%	8.8%
25% percentile	39.9%	7.3%	29.9%	6.5%	24.7%	6.9%
75% percentile	59.2%	10.0%	39.3%	8.0%	36.1%	10.8%
Beta: 1.34/1.49 To 1.95/1.99 (2nd Quintile)						
No. of companies	113		107		126	
Mean	46.4%	8.3%	29.6%	6.8%	26.2%	6.3%
Median	43.3%	7.4%	28.8%	7.4%	24.1%	6.7%
25% percentile	35.9%	5.9%	25.2%	5.9%	22.1%	6.2%
75% percentile	51.4%	8.6%	32.3%	8.0%	28.3%	7.4%
Beta: 1.00/1.12 To 1.34/1.49 (3rd Quintile)						
No. of companies	145		120		132	
Mean	42.2%	6.9%	26.6%	5.9%	24.7%	6.9%
Median	40.2%	6.7%	25.2%	5.7%	22.0%	6.0%
25% percentile	34.2%	6.3%	23.2%	5.5%	20.1%	5.5%
75% percentile	47.6%	7.7%	28.7%	6.6%	25.7%	7.0%
Beta: 0.66/0.77 To 1.00/1.12 (4th Quintile)						
No. of companies	121		120		132	
Mean	39.9%	7.4%	26.2%	6.7%	22.6%	6.5%
Median	37.1%	6.3%	23.3%	5.6%	20.7%	6.0%
25% percentile	31.5%	6.8%	20.5%	5.8%	18.4%	5.3%
75% percentile	45.0%	7.1%	27.7%	6.8%	25.0%	7.7%
Beta: Negative To 0.66/0.77 (5th Quintile)						
No. of companies	125		119		129	
Mean	37.2%	4.5%	22.9%	5.2%	22.0%	5.8%
Median	35.5%	5.6%	20.4%	4.9%	19.4%	5.9%
25% percentile	27.0%	4.5%	18.1%	4.8%	17.0%	5.4%
75% percentile	42.6%	4.3%	25.2%	5.5%	23.4%	4.5%

* The measure "Incr. *" is the absolute percentage increase in discount of the longer term LEAPS over the shorter term LEAPS; i.e., the cost of an additional 12 months of price protection.

Note: In our study of September 2007, titled "Minimum Marketability Discounts - 3rd Edition," the cost of price protection by company betas was studied. However, the source of the betas and the calculations were not comparable to later studies. The results were similar but are not shown here.

As with the discussion of dividends, the question arises whether, or to what extent, betas are a function of company size; that is, is a discount for beta duplicative of a discount for company size? The following chart suggests that, as a broad generality, betas are lower for companies with larger revenues. This seems intuitively logical because larger companies typically are older and more stable in their life cycles. However, the ranges of revenue size within each beta quintile are so wide that it is clear that individual company risk conditions effect beta much more than sheer size. The fact that quintiles 1 and 2, with betas above 1.47, contain companies with revenues over $156 billion (Bank of America and General Electric, respectively) demonstrates this.

Company Revenue Size As A Function of Beta
(dollars in billlions)

Beta	Average	Median	25th %	75th %	Highest	Lowest
1.95 and Higher (1st Quintile)	$8,345.0	$2,955.4	$845.1	$7,763.0	$150,450.0	$0.0
1.47 Through 1.94 (2nd Quintile)	$8,886.3	$2,775.1	$664.7	$9,530.3	$156,783.0	$0.0
1.11 Through 1.46 (3rd Quintile)	$15,473.7	$3,879.9	$941.9	$14,170.0	$239,272.0	$0.0
0.74 Through 1.10 (4th Quintile)	$15,419.4	$4,880.6	$1,788.3	$15,602.9	$188,423.0	$9.3
Neg. To 0.74 (5th Quintile)	$21,900.5	$5,682.0	$1,507.4	$18,031.0	$408,214.0	$0.0

For the practicing business valuator, beta is a significant indicator of the size of a DLOM. We suggest that a company's beta, or a comparable estimate of market risk, be included in the analysis of a final discount conclusion using a Mandelbaum grid as is described later in this book.

COST OF PRICE PROTECTION AS A FUNCTION OF PROFIT MARGIN: 2010 STUDY

Profit margin is calculated as Net Income After Tax (NIAT) available to common shareholders divided by Total Revenues, both measured at the latest year end. The calculation of quintiles in Chart IX is based on 2012 options. Because some companies do not offer 2013 options, the 2013 counts will be less.

As Chart IX shows, costs of price protection decrease as profit margin increases. The differences are more pronounced as profit margins become negative (i.e., losses). The averages and medians of the top three quartiles (the profitable companies) are quite similar, and the ranges of the middle 50%'s vary from 5% to 7%. Thus, the degree of profitability does not appear to be a significant determinant of the cost of price protection. Borderline profitability or losses clearly do increase the discount. In contrast, it is interesting to note that the range of the middle 50% of quintile 5 (losses of 3.6% or more) varies by 13.7%. In addition, the cost of the additional 12 months of price protection also increases as companies become less profitable.

Chart IX
Costs of Price Protection By Profit Margin: 2010

Months To Expiration of Option	13 1/2	25 1/2	
	2012 Option	2013 Option	Incr.* '13-'12
Profit Margins: 14.7% and Higher (1st Quintile)			
Count	155	131	
Average	17.0%	23.4%	6.3%
Median	15.3%	20.9%	5.6%
25th Percentile	13.3%	18.6%	5.3%
75th Percentile	18.9%	25.6%	6.7%
Profit Margins: 7.9% To 14.6% (2nd Quintile)			
Count	155	133	
Average	15.8%	22.2%	6.4%
Median	15.4%	21.4%	6.0%
25th Percentile	13.0%	19.2%	6.2%
75th Percentile	17.8%	24.6%	6.8%
Profit Margins: 3.1% Through 7.8% (3rd Quintile)			
Count	155	136	
Average	16.2%	22.8%	6.7%
Median	15.4%	21.8%	6.5%
25th Percentile	13.2%	18.8%	5.6%
75th Percentile	17.8%	25.1%	7.3%
Profit Margins: Neg. 3.6% Through 3.0% (4th Quintile)			
Count	155	126	
Average	18.7%	26.2%	7.5%
Median	17.7%	24.5%	6.8%
25th Percentile	15.8%	21.6%	5.8%
75th Percentile	21.0%	29.1%	8.1%
Profit Margins: Greater Negatives Than 3.6%			
Count	154	124	
Average	25.1%	35.5%	10.4%
Median	22.6%	29.9%	7.3%
25th Percentile	17.8%	24.1%	6.3%
75th Percentile	27.9%	37.8%	9.9%

Survey data from early December 2010.

Note: Profit margins calculated as Net Income After Taxes attributable to common shareholders divided by Revenues. Both NIAT and Revenues are from the latest full year financials available, typically the full year 2009.

* "Incr. '13>'12" is the absolute percentage increase in the discount for an additional 12 months of time; that is, the time from the shorter term discount, 13 1/2 months for the shorter term 2012 option, to 25 1/2 months for the 2013 option.

Cost of Price Protection As A Function of Profit Margin: Annual Comparisons

Chart X shows the same characteristics during each of the past two years.[14] That is, similar costs of price protection for profitable companies; companies with losses requiring higher discounts; and the cost of the additional 12 months increasing as profitability decreases. As in the earlier analyses, discounts were uniformly lower in 2010 than in 2009.

The 2007 study included analysis of the effect on discounts of a company's 5-year, average, annual, earnings growth using data from Standard and Poor's <u>Stock</u> <u>Guide</u>. The results were about the same as those of the profit margin studies. Discounts in a central range, defined by S & P as from positive average annual growth to 99% per year to an average annual decline up to -49% per year, were very similar. At either extreme, annual average profits above 99% per year or annual average declines greater than 49% per year, increased discounts. However, there were no other patterns that are useful to appraisers.

---

14 Our studies included the profit margin percentage only in the past two years (those shown in Chart X). The first study, in 2007, included profit margin percentage using different criteria (than quintiles), so the data is not comparable. However, the conclusions from the data are very similar.

Chart X
Costs of Price Protection By Profit Margin: Annual Comparisons

Date of Survey Data Months To Option Expiration	November 2009 26		December 2010 25 1/2	
	2012 Option	Increase* '12 >'11	2013 Option	Increase 13>'12
Profit Margins:15.4%/14.7% and Higher (1st Quintile)				
Count	116		131	
Average	24.6%	5.9%	23.4%	6.3%
Median	24.0%	5.5%	20.9%	5.6%
25th Percentile	20.9%	5.4%	18.6%	5.3%
75th Percentile	27.5%	6.3%	25.6%	6.7%
Profit Margins: 7.9%/8.2% To 14.6%/15.3% (2nd Quintile)				
Count	124		133	
Average	24.4%	6.1%	22.2%	6.4%
Median	23.6%	5.4%	21.4%	6.0%
25th Percentile	19.2%	4.8%	19.2%	6.2%
75th Percentile	28.4%	7.2%	24.6%	6.8%
Profit Margins: 3.1%/3.5% Through 7.8%/8.1% (3rd Quintile)				
Count	111		136	
Average	25.6%	5.5%	22.8%	6.7%
Median	24.3%	5.5%	21.8%	6.5%
25th Percentile	21.3%	5.4%	18.8%	5.6%
75th Percentile	29.0%	6.3%	25.1%	7.3%
Profit Margins: Neg. 3.6%/6.6% Through 3.0%/3.5% (4th Quintile)				
Count	110		126	
Average	29.0%	6.1%	26.2%	7.5%
Median	28.4%	7.1%	24.5%	6.8%
25th Percentile	23.7%	5.0%	21.6%	5.8%
75th Percentile	32.1%	7.0%	29.1%	8.1%
Profit Margins: Greater Negatives Than 3.6%/6.7% (5th Quintile)				
Count	111		124	
Average	35.2%	7.8%	35.5%	10.4%
Median	32.6%	7.2%	29.9%	7.3%
25th Percentile	27.9%	6.7%	24.1%	6.3%
75th Percentile	39.6%	8.1%	37.8%	9.9%

* "Incr. '13>'12" is the absolute percentage increase in the discount for an additional
12 months of time; that is, the time from the shorter term discount, 13 1/2 months for
the shorter term 2012 option, to 25 1/2 months for the 2013 option.

Note: In our study of September 2007, titled "Minimum Marketability Discounts - 3rd Edition,"
the cost of price protection by profit margin was studied. The format in which the data
was collected was different; therefore, the results are not shown here although the
conclusions were very similar.

Cost of Price Protection As A Function of Debt/ Equity Ratio: 2010 Study

As Chart XI indicates, the Debt/Equity ratio is defined as Total Liabilities divided by Shareholders Equity available to common shares. The quintiles are based on the 2012 option, so each quintile has fewer companies with 2013 options. The results are much like those when analyzing the profit margin: costs of price protection in the central quintiles, 2, 3 and 4, are fairly homogeneous, while the lower and higher quintiles require higher discounts. The cost of an additional 12 months of price protection shows the same pattern.

However, the debt/equity ratio is not a major determinant of discounts because the 25th percentile in either quintile 1 or quintile 5 (the extremes) is close to the medians of the other quintiles. In addition, the medians in each of the five quintiles have a narrow range, from 22.0% to 25.8%. Thus, for the business valuation practitioner determining a DLOM, the debt/equity ratio of the subject company can be a contributing factor to a conclusion but probably not a dominant factor unless it is unusually high or low.

Chart XI
Costs of Price Protection By Debt/Equity Ratio: 2010 Study

	2012 Option	2013 Option	Increase 13>'12
Debt/Equity Ratio: 3.3 and Higher (1st Quintile)			
Count	154	141	
Average	18.6%	27.0%	8.4%
Median	16.8%	23.8%	7.0%
25th Percentile	14.7%	20.5%	5.8%
75th Percentile	21.1%	29.9%	8.8%
Debt/Equity Ration: 1.6 to 3.3 (2nd Quintile)			
Count	154	128	
Average	17.2%	23.0%	5.8%
Median	15.8%	22.0%	6.2%
25th Percentile	13.1%	18.7%	5.6%
75th Percentile	18.8%	25.5%	6.7%
Debt/Equity Ratio: 0.9 to 1.6 (3rd Quintile)			
Count	154	123	
Average	16.6%	23.5%	6.9%
Median	15.9%	22.2%	6.2%
25th Percentile	13.5%	19.2%	5.7%
75th Percentile	18.9%	26.2%	7.3%
Debt/Equity Ratio: 0.4 to 0.9 (4th Quintile)			
Count	154	131	
Average	18.3%	25.0%	6.8%
Median	16.3%	22.4%	6.1%
25th Percentile	14.3%	19.3%	5.0%
75th Percentile	20.9%	28.0%	7.1%
Debt/Equity Ratio: Neg. to 0.4 (5th Quintile) (a)			
Count	155	125	
Average	22.0%	30.6%	8.6%
Median	18.9%	25.8%	6.9%
25th Percentile	15.9%	21.4%	5.5%
75th Percentile	24.2%	33.3%	9.0%

* "Incr. '13>'12" is the absolute percentage increase in the discount for an additional 12 months of time; that is, the time from the shorter term discount, 13 1/2 months for the shorter term 2012 option, to 25 1/2 months for the 2013 option.

* Debt/Equity Ratio calculated as "Total Liabilities" ÷ "Shareholders' Equity."

(a) Negative debt/equity ratios are caused by negative equity positions.

Cost of Price Protection As A Function of Debt/ Equity Ratio: Annual Comparisons

The study of debt/equity ratios has only been done in 2009 and 2010, so comparisons with earlier years do not exist. The comparison of results in the 2009 and 2010 studies (Chart XII) shows essentially the same facts as the 2010 study alone. The middle three quintiles have quite similar medians, averages, ranges of the middle 50% and increased costs for an additional 12 months, while the 1st and 5th quintiles have higher discounts. The debt/equity ratio can be a contributing factor in reaching a DLOM decision but it is not likely to be a dominant factor unless unusually high or low.

Chart XII

Costs of Price Protection By Debt/Equity Ratio; Annual Comparisons

Date of Survey Data	November 2009		December 2010	
Months To Option Expiration	26		25 1/2	
	2012 Option	Incr. * 12 > '11	2013 Option	Incr. * 13>'12
Debt/Equity Ratio: 3.3/3.8 and Higher (1st Quintile)				
Count	114		141	
Average	30.1%	7.0%	27.0%	8.4%
Median	29.0%	6.6%	23.8%	7.0%
25th Percentile	23.6%	5.6%	20.5%	5.8%
75th Percentile	33.7%	7.1%	29.9%	8.8%
Debt/Equity Ration: 1.6/1.9 to 3.3/3.7 (2nd Quintile)				
Count	108		128	
Average	27.3%	6.1%	23.0%	5.8%
Median	25.0%	5.4%	22.0%	6.2%
25th Percentile	20.6%	5.3%	18.7%	5.6%
75th Percentile	31.5%	6.8%	25.5%	6.7%
Debt/Equity Ratio: 0.9/1.2 to 1.6/1.9 (3rd Quintile)				
Count	112		123	
Average	26.9%	5.9%	23.5%	6.9%
Median	25.5%	5.3%	22.2%	6.2%
25th Percentile	21.7%	5.4%	19.2%	5.7%
75th Percentile	31.8%	8.5%	26.2%	7.3%
Debt/Equity Ratio: 0.4/0.6 to 0.9/1.2 (4th Quintile)				
Count	116		131	
Average	25.0%	4.9%	25.0%	6.8%
Median	24.0%	5.3%	22.4%	6.1%
25th Percentile	20.2%	5.0%	19.3%	5.0%
75th Percentile	28.3%	6.1%	28.0%	7.1%
Debt/Equity Ratio: Neg. to 0.4/0.6 (5th Quintile) (a)				
Count	106		125	
Average	28.9%	7.0%	30.6%	8.6%
Median	26.3%	6.1%	25.8%	6.9%
25th Percentile	23.3%	5.5%	21.4%	5.5%
75th Percentile	30.7%	6.3%	33.3%	9.0%

* Debt/Equity Ration calculated as "Total Liabilities" divided by "Shareholders' Equity." Financial data are from the latest full year financials available.

(a) Negative debt/equity ratios are caused by negative equity positions.

Note: Studies prior to November 2009 did not contain an analysis of the costs of price protection by debt/equity ratios.

Cost of Price Protection As A Function of % Return On Equity: 2010 Study

A company's percentage return on equity is calculated as net income after taxes (NIAT) available to common shareholders divided by common shareholders' equity, both at the latest year end. Chart XIII shows the costs of price protection in the 2010 study. The quintile breaks are interesting by themselves, with 20% of companies having returns on equity greater than 21.1% and 20% having negative returns on equity greater than -4.3%. Perhaps this is not unusual considering economic conditions in 2009 which usually was the latest full year reported as of December 2010. Nevertheless, the top three quintiles, companies with returns on equity of 5.8% or greater, warranted quite similar discounts: averages and medians in the range of 21% to 23% for 25 ½ months of price protection (the 2013 option). Also, for the top three quintiles, ranges of the middle 50% of companies and costs of the additional 12 months of price protection (the "Incr." column) were quite similar.

In the bottom two quintiles, as returns on equity decreased and became negative, discounts increased, more noticeably as the loss became greater. For negative returns on equity greater than 4.3%, the median cost of price protection for the 2013 option was 28.9% and the middle 50% ranged from 23% to 37%.

Thus, a company's percentage return on equity certainly is a factor that influences the DLOM conclusion but is often not a dominant factor. Its influence on the DLOM conclusion is likely to be greater as it becomes unusually low.

Chart XIII
Costs of Price Protection By % Return On Equity

Months To Expiration of Option	13 1/2	25 1/2	
	2012 Option	2013 Option	Incr. * 13>'12
Returns on Equity: 21.1% and Higher (1st Quintile)			
Count	155	133	
Average	14.2%	23.5%	9.3%
Median	15.4%	21.3%	5.9%
25th Percentile	12.7%	18.2%	5.5%
75th Percentile	20.3%	27.2%	6.8%
Returns on Equity: 12.5% To 21.2% (2nd Quintile)			
Count	155	134	
Average	15.8%	22.7%	6.9%
Median	14.8%	20.6%	5.8%
25th Percentile	13.2%	18.7%	5.5%
75th Percentile	17.0%	23.5%	6.6%
Returns on Equity: 5.8% Through 12.4% (3rd Quintile)			
Count	155	131	
Average	16.6%	23.2%	6.6%
Median	16.1%	22.2%	6.1%
25th Percentile	13.6%	19.5%	5.8%
75th Percentile	18.2%	25.2%	6.9%
Returns on Equity: Neg. 4.1% to 5.8% (4th Quintile)			
Count	154	130	
Average	18.5%	25.8%	7.3%
Median	17.4%	24.4%	7.0%
25th Percentile	15.9%	21.4%	5.5%
75th Percentile	20.7%	28.3%	7.6%
Returns on Equity: Greater than -4.3% (5th Quintile)			
Count	155	122	
Average	23.8%	34.1%	10.3%
Median	21.6%	28.9%	7.3%
25th Percentile	17.4%	23.0%	5.6%
75th Percentile	27.2%	36.8%	9.7%

* "Incr. '13>'12" is the absolute percentage increase in the discount for an additional
12 months of time; that is, the time from the shorter term discount, 13 1/2 months for
the shorter term 2012 option, to 25 1/2 months for the 2013 option.

Cost of Price Protection As A Function of % Return on Equity: Annual Comparisons

As Chart XIV shows, costs of price protection were uniformly lower in December 2010 than in November 2009. However, the patterns among the quintiles were the same. The three quintiles with the highest returns on equity had quite similar costs of price protection, while lower or negative returns on equity clearly caused higher discounts.

Chart XIV
Costs of Price Protection By % Return on Equity

Date of Survey Data Months To Option Expiration	November 2009 26		December 2010 25 1/2	
	2012 Option	Incr. * 12 > '11	2013 Option	Incr.* 13>'12
ROE: Greater Than 25.0%/21.1% (1st Quintile)				
Count	116		133	
Average	23.9%	5.9%	23.5%	9.3%
Median	23.3%	5.5%	21.3%	5.9%
25th Percentile	19.1%	4.8%	18.2%	5.5%
75th Percentile	27.8%	6.9%	27.2%	6.8%
ROE: 12.5%/15.4% To 21.1%/24.8% (2nd Quintile)				
Count	122		134	
Average	24.8%	5.9%	22.7%	6.9%
Median	24.2%	5.8%	20.6%	5.8%
25th Percentile	21.2%	5.7%	18.7%	5.5%
75th Percentile	27.5%	5.9%	23.5%	6.6%
ROE: 5.8%/7.0% To 12.4%.15.4% (3rd Quintile)				
Count	106		131	
Average	25.3%	5.8%	23.2%	6.6%
Median	24.2%	5.5%	22.2%	6.1%
25th Percentile	20.6%	5.2%	19.5%	5.8%
75th Percentile	28.3%	6.6%	25.2%	6.9%
ROE: Neg. 4..1%/11.4% To 5.8%/6.9% (4th Quintile)				
Count	100		130	
Average	29.2%	6.5%	25.8%	7.3%
Median	28.7%	6.9%	24.4%	7.0%
25th Percentile	24.9%	5.8%	21.4%	5.5%
75th Percentile	32.6%	7.4%	28.3%	7.6%
ROE: Greater Negatives Than 4.3%/11.4% (5th Quintile)				
Count	107		122	
Average	35.3%	7.5%	34.1%	10.3%
Median	32.7%	6.9%	28.9%	7.3%
25th Percentile	27.6%	6.4%	23.0%	5.6%
75th Percentile	39.6%	7.9%	36.8%	9.7%

* "Incr. '13>'12" is the absolute percentage increase in the discount for an additional
12 months of time; that is, the time from the shorter term discount, 13 1/2 months for
the shorter term 2012 option, to 25 1/2 months for the 2013 option.

Note: Earlier studies than those shown above did not contain an analysis of the cost
of price protection by returns on equity.

LEAPS STUDIES: INDUSTRY CHARACTERISTICS

In 2008 we began to study the costs of price protection by industry and by sub-category within industries using the "Industry" definitions of Yahoo Finance. Yahoo Finance defines nine industries: Basic Materials, Conglomerates, Consumer Goods, Financial, Healthcare, Industrial Goods, Services, Technology and Utilities. Chart XV shows the discounts/costs of price protection on the longer term option (24 months and longer) for each of those industries for the last three years.

It is very clear that discounts peaked in 2008 and have come down dramatically since. In 2008 industry medians ranged from 26.8% to 43.7%. In 2010 they ranged from 16.4% to 24.6%. Yet, in each year, the medians and ranges of the middle 50% of discounts in each industry were quite similar to the medians and ranges of all companies as a group. For example, in 2010, the median cost of price protection for all 650 companies studied was 23.0%. Excluding the seven "Conglomerates" and the thirteen "Utilities," the remaining seven "Industries" in 2010 had median discounts from 21.9% to 24.6%, a narrow range and very similar to the median of all 650 companies (23.0%). However, a study of the ranges of the middle 50% of companies in each industry shows that the ranges are wide varying from 20% to 50% of the median. For example, in 2010 the median discount in the "Healthcare" industry is 22.2%, while the range of the middle 50% of companies in the industry is from 18.7% to 37.3%. Thus, the breakdown into nine "Industries" does not contribute much to arriving at a DLOM conclusion for any specific company. A more detailed definition is required.

Chart XV
Costs of Price Protection By Industry Sector

Date of Survey Data Months To Expiration	November 2008 26		November 2009 26		December 2010 25 1/2	
Sector	2011 Option	Incr.* '11 > '10	2012 Option	Incr.* '12 >'11	2013 Option	Incr.* '13 >'12
1 Basic Materials						
No. of companies	110		105		126	
Mean	44.4%	5.8%	28.3%	6.4%	25.7%	7.1%
Median	42.0%	6.0%	27.5%	6.5%	23.4%	6.6%
25% percentile	38.2%	6.6%	24.0%	5.5%	21.4%	5.8%
75% percentile	49.8%	7.7%	32.0%	7.4%	26.6%	6.9%
2 Conglomerates						
No. of companies	5		5		7	
Mean	32.1%	0.9%	21.4%	6.0%	17.6%	5.0%
Median	26.8%	2.2%	20.6%	6.2%	16.4%	4.8%
25% percentile	26.5%	5.3%	18.0%	4.7%	15.6%	4.2%
75% percentile	35.3%	2.6%	22.7%	6.0%	18.8%	5.6%
3 Consumer Goods						
No. of companies	52		48		53	
Mean	40.5%	5.9%	25.3%	5.2%	23.3%	6.1%
Median	36.9%	6.0%	23.6%	4.8%	21.9%	6.1%
25% percentile	26.6%	2.5%	19.0%	4.7%	19.0%	5.9%
75% percentile	48.8%	7.9%	28.9%	5.4%	27.3%	6.4%
4 Financial						
No. of companies	69		61		79	
Mean	49.6%	8.0%	30.0%	6.6%	26.6%	8.2%
Median	43.7%	5.8%	28.3%	7.0%	22.8%	6.4%
25% percentile	39.2%	7.5%	24.9%	6.3%	20.6%	5.7%
75% percentile	54.7%	10.2%	33.3%	7.7%	25.8%	7.2%
5 Healthcare						
No. of companies	72		68		63	
Mean	41.8%	5.3%	30.8%	7.1%	32.7%	9.7%
Median	38.2%	5.7%	24.6%	5.2%	22.2%	5.0%
25% percentile	28.1%	4.2%	19.4%	5.0%	18.7%	5.2%
75% percentile	51.5%	6.8%	31.6%	2.8%	37.3%	9.4%
6 Industrial Goods						
No. of companies	48		46		42	
Mean	42.9%	7.6%	28.1%	6.7%	24.9%	6.8%
Median	40.1%	6.6%	27.3%	6.2%	22.9%	6.2%
25% percentile	33.9%	7.2%	22.6%	5.9%	20.3%	6.7%
75% percentile	50.6%	8.9%	31.5%	6.7%	27.6%	8.5%

Chart XV (cont'd)
Costs of Price Protection By Industry Sector

Date of Survey Data Months To Expiration	November 2008 26		November 2009 26		December 2010 25 1/2	
	2011 Option	Incr.* '11 > '10	2012 Option	Incr.* '12 >'11	2013 Option	Incr.* '13 >'12
7 Services						
No. of companies	126		115		128	
Mean	45.0%	7.9%	27.0%	5.7%	24.7%	7.2%
Median	41.9%	8.0%	25.7%	5.4%	23.1%	6.3%
25% percentile	34.1%	6.1%	20.7%	4.8%	19.3%	5.8%
75% percentile	54.8%	11.5%	31.6%	7.1%	28.5%	7.6%
8 Technology						
No. of companies	129		117		139	
Mean	40.7%	6.2%	26.9%	5.8%	25.5%	7.2%
Median	37.5%	5.5%	25.6%	5.9%	24.6%	6.8%
25% percentile	33.2%	6.0%	21.7%	4.9%	20.0%	5.3%
75% percentile	46.2%	7.1%	31.0%	7.0%	29.1%	8.2%
9 Utilities						
No. of companies	12		12		13	
Mean	32.5%	7.2%	26.3%	7.7%	23.2%	8.3%
Median	28.6%	4.9%	22.1%	6.8%	19.2%	6.0%
25% percentile	25.3%	4.4%	19.4%	6.0%	17.7%	6.5%
75% percentile	35.6%	10.3%	27.3%	6.8%	22.3%	7.1%

* "Increase" is the absolute percentage increase in the discount for an additional 12 months of time; that is, the time from the shorter term discount, 13 1/2 months for a 2012 option, to 25 1/2 months for the 2013 option.

Technology Industry

Breaking down the nine "Industries" into sub-categories provides much more guidance. Charts XVI and XVII show the 32 sub-categories into which Yahoo Finance divides the "Technology Industry" ranging from "Application Software" to Wireless Communications." In December 2010, there are a total of 139 technology companies with LEAPS. Of the 32 possible sub-categories, 28 have companies whose LEAPS trade publicly. Chart XVI shows each sub-category in each of the last three survey years. For "All Companies" in the industry, the costs of price protection/discounts are down since 2008. The November 2009 survey's discounts are significantly lower than 2008, and those in December 2010 are somewhat lower than 2009.

However, there are important differences in discounts in the various sub-categories of the industry. Note that, in December 2010, average discounts for the sub-categories range from 17% - 18% at the low end to 33% - 34% at the upper end. The average discount for 9 companies in the "Application Software" sub-category is 19.4%, while the average discount for 15 companies in the "Semiconductor – Specialized" sub-category is 29.9%. In addition, the range of the middle 50% of companies in each sub-category is significant. For example, in "Application Software" the range of the middle 50% of companies (from the median) is 0.6%; for "Semiconductor – Specialized," the range is 15.1%. For the practicing business appraiser, these facts simply point out the importance of defining the industry comparison base in as much detail as possible before reaching a DLOM conclusion. Differences among companies in their costs of price protection can be wide and justifying your use of the data is important.

Chart XVI
Technology Industry
Costs of Price Protection By Industry Sub-Category

Date of Survey Data	Nov. 2008	Nov. 2009	Dec. 2010
Months To Expiration	26	26	25 1/2
	2011 Option	2012 Option	2013 Option
All Companies			
Count	129	117	139
Average	40.7%	26.9%	25.5%
Median	37.5%	25.6%	24.6%
25th Percentile	30.2%	21.7%	20.0%
75th Percentile	46.2%	31.0%	29.1%
Sub-Cat. 1 - Application Software			
Count	10	11	9
Average	33.2%	21.3%	19.4%
Median	32.1%	20.7%	18.6%
25th Percentile	30.0%	18.5%	18.3%
75th Percentile	34.2%	22.6%	18.9%
Sub-Cat. 2 - Business Software & Services			
Count	4	5	5
Average	32.4%	26.1%	25.1%
Median	33.0%	22.2%	21.8%
25th Percentile		21.6%	20.5%
75th Percentile		34.5%	33.2%
Sub-Cat. 3 - Communication Equipment			
Count	11	11	10
Average	42.3%	29.1%	27.1%
Median	44.1%	28.0%	26.3%
25th Percentile	37.1%	24.5%	21.9%
75th Percentile	47.4%	31.9%	29.4%
Sub-Cat. 4 - Computer Based Systems			
Count			1
Average			25.1%
Sub-Cat. 5 - Computer Peripherals			
Count	1	1	2
Average	27.3%	22.9%	24.8%

Chart XVI (cont'd)
Technology Industry
Costs of Price Protection By Industry Sub-Category

Date of Survey Data	Nov. 2008	Nov. 2009	Dec. 2010
Months To Expiration	26	26	25 1/2
Sub-Cat. 6 - Data Storage Devices			
Count	5	5	7
Average	38.5%	23.9%	21.6%
Median	36.3%	24.2%	22.5%
25th Percentile	36.3%	22.9%	20.0%
75th Percentile	40.4%	26.4%	24.2%
Sub-Cat. 7 - Diversified Communication Services			
Count	3	1	1
Average	33.5%	20.9%	17.1%
Median	34.0%		
Sub-Cat. 8 - Diversified Computer Systems			
Count	4	4	3
Average	34.7%	19.3%	19.6%
Median	33.1%	17.9%	17.6%
Sub-Cat. 9 - Diversified Electronics			
Count	5	1	2
Average	59.6%	37.5%	34.2%
Median	64.5%		
25th Percentile	50.7%		
75th Percentile	71.0%		
Sub-Cat. 10 - Healthcare Information Systems			
Count			1
Average			18.4%
Sub-Cat. 12 - Information Technology Services			
Count			4
Average			27.5%
Median			29.5%
Sub-Cat. 13 - Internet Information Providers			
Count	7	8	6
Average	38.9%	24.6%	23.5%
Median	42.0%	25.7%	24.8%
25th Percentile	35.5%	24.6%	20.6%
75th Percentile	43.5%	26.4%	25.9%

Chart XVI (cont'd)
Technology Industry
Costs of Price Protection By Industry Sub-Category

Date of Survey Data Months To Expiration	Nov. 2008 26	Nov. 2009 26	Dec. 2010 25 1/2
Sub-Cat. 15 - Internet Software and Services			
Count	10	3	5
Average	36.6%	32.0%	33.0%
Median	35.4%	33.1%	26.6%
25th Percentile	32.8%	29.0%	26.0%
75th Percentile	36.3%	35.6%	32.9%
Sub-Cat. 17 - Multilmedia and Graphics Software			
Count	3	2	3
Average	42.1%	28.3%	23.3%
Median	39.6%		22.1%
Sub-Cat. 18 - Networking & Communication Devices			
Count	3	4	5
Average	35.0%	24.0%	23.8%
Median	33.0%	23.9%	23.6%
25th Percentile			22.7%
75th Percentile			24.9%
Sub-Cat. 19 - Personal Computers			
Count	2	3	2
Average	35.6%	28.8%	20.0%
Median		23.4%	
Sub-Cat. 20 - Printed Circuit Boards			
Count	2	2	2
Average	52.1%	30.6%	29.6%
Sub-Cat. 22 - Scientific & Technical Instruments			
Count	3	2	3
Average	37.3%	25.5%	23.4%
Median	37.8%		23.9%
Sub-Cat. 23 - Security Software & Services			
Count	2	3	4
Average	29.3%	19.5%	19.7%
Median		20.2%	19.9%

Chart XVI (cont'd)
Technology Industry
Costs of Price Protection By Industry Sub-Category

Date of Survey Data	Nov. 2008	Nov. 2009	Dec. 2010
Months To Expiration	26	26	25 1/2

Sub-Cat. 24 - Semiconductor - Broad Line

Count	7	7	11
Average	37.9%	26.2%	28.6%
Median	35.8%	27.1%	26.1%
25th Percentile	33.0%	21.6%	22.7%
75th Percentile	37.7%	29.3%	32.1%

Sub-Cat. 25 - Semiconductor - Integrated Circuits

Count	7	10	12
Average	50.4%	30.2%	27.8%
Median	44.3%	29.6%	25.7%
25th Percentile	40.3%	25.9%	23.7%
75th Percentile	60.9%	31.7%	30.5%

Sub-Cat. 26 - Semiconductor - Specialized

Count	11	12	15
Average	45.4%	31.9%	29.9%
Median	42.4%	32.9%	26.4%
25th Percentile	33.8%	23.7%	21.2%
75th Percentile	48.3%	36.7%	36.3%

Sub-Cat. 27 - Semiconductor Equipment & Materials

Count	8	7	6
Average	39.9%	25.6%	24.0%
Median	39.5%	23.9%	22.9%
25th Percentile	36.9%	23.2%	21.4%
75th Percentile	43.1%	27.3%	25.0%

Sub-Cat. 28 - Semiconductor - Memory Chips

Count	4	4	4
Average	54.4%	34.2%	28.0%
Median	58.3%	31.8%	29.8%

Sub-Cat. 29 - Technical & System Software

Count	3	2	2
Average	40.1%	26.7%	25.1%
Median	39.5		

Chart XVI (cont'd)
Technology Industry
Costs of Price Protection By Industry Sub-Category

Date of Survey Data	Nov. 2008	Nov. 2009	Dec. 2010
Months To Expiration	26	26	25 1/2
Sub-Cat. 30 - Telecom Services - Domestic			
Count	4	2	6
Average	33.9%	21.1%	24.2%
Median	33.1%		21.8%
25th Percentile			19.3%
75th Percentile			26.8%
Sub-Cat. 31 - Telecom Services - Foreign			
Count	1		1
Average	38.7%		18.4%
Sub-Cat. 32 - Wireless Communications			
Count	7	7	7
Average	46.0%	29.2%	24.2%
Median	44.4%	29.0%	25.7%
25th Percentile	39.0%	25.5%	21.8%
75th Percentile	53.5%	32.5%	26.8%

Chart XVII summarizes the costs of price protection as shown by the 2013 put option for each sub-category of the "Technology Industry." The differences between the Industry sub-categories are evident.

Chart XVII
Technology Industry
Costs of Price Protection: 2013 Option
(As of December 2010)

		Count	Mean	Median	Range of Mid.-50% *
1	Application Software	9	19.4%	18.6%	0.6%
2	Business Software & Services	5	25.1%	21.8%	12.7%
3	Communication Equipment	10	27.1%	26.3%	7.5%
4	Computer-Based Systems	1	25.1%		
5	Computer Peripherals	2	24.8%		
6	Data Storage Devices	7	21.6%	22.5%	4.2%
7	Diversified Communication Services	1	17.1%		
8	Diversified Computer Systems	3	19.6%	17.6%	
9	Diversified Electronics	2	34.2%		
10	Healthcare Information Systems	1	18.4%		
12	Information Technology Services	4	27.5%	29.5%	
13	Internet Information Providers	6	23.5%	24.8%	5.3%
15	Internet Software and Services	5	33.0%	26.6%	6.9%
17	Multilmedia and Graphics Software	3	23.3%	22.1%	
18	Networking & Communication Devices	5	23.8%	23.6%	2.2%
19	Personal Computers	2	20.0%		
20	Printed Circuit Boards	2	29.6%		
22	Scientific & Technical Instruments	3	23.4%	23.9%	
23	Security Software & Services	4	19.7%	19.9%	
24	Semiconductor - Broad Line	11	28.6%	26.1%	9.4%
25	Semiconductor - Integrated Circuits	12	27.8%	25.7%	6.8%
26	Semiconductor - Specialized	15	29.9%	26.4%	15.1%
27	Semiconductor Equipment & Materials	6	24.0%	22.9%	3.6%
28	Semiconductor - Memory Chips	4	28.0%	29.8%	
29	Technical & System Software	2	25.1%		
30	Telecom Services - Domestic	6	24.2%	21.8%	7.5%
31	Telecom Services - Foreign	1	18.4%		
32	Wireless Communications	7	24.2%	25.7%	5.0%

* Cost of price protection at the 75th percentile minus the cost of price protection at the 25th percentile.

Within the "Healthcare Industry" Yahoo Finance defines 16 sub-categories. 13 of these sub-categories, 63 separate companies, have LEAPS publicly traded. Chart XVIII shows the costs of price protection for the 24-month plus put option in each sub-category in each of the last three years. As with all of the other industries, discounts dropped substantially in 2009 from 2008 and dropped again, but in much smaller increments, in 2010.

As with the "Technology Industry," the results from all 63 companies (the industry as a whole) are not very useful for a particular appraisal assignment (unless no better source is available) because the results in the sub-categories vary so much. For example, the median discount in December 2010 for the eight, "Drug Manufacturers – Major" is 19.5%, and the range of the middle 50% of companies in that sub-category is from 18.9% to 20.1% - a narrow range of results. The "Biotechnology" sub-category is very different: a median cost of price protection of 36.7% and a range of the middle 50% of companies from 22.0% to 56.6%! Sub-category 8 – 'Healthcare Plans' has a very narrow range of discounts, while Sub-category 5 – "Drug Manufacturers – Other" has a much wider range.

Chart XVIII
Healthcare Industry
Costs of Price Protection By Industry Sub-Category

Date of Survey Data Months To Expiration	Nov. 2008 26	Nov. 2009 26	Dec. 2010 25 1/2
	2011 Option	2012 Option	2013 Option
All Companies			
Count	72	68	63
Average	41.8%	30.8%	32.7%
Median	38.2%	24.6%	22.2%
25th Percentile	28.1%	19.4%	18.7%
75th Percentile	51.5%	31.6%	37.3%
Sub-Cat. 1 - Biotechnology			
Count	23	19	20
Average	53.9%	40.5%	40.5%
Median	51.6%	31.0%	36.7%
25th Percentile	34.2%	21.1%	22.0%
75th Percentile	69.1%	51.1%	56.6%
Sub-Cat. 2 - Diagnostic Substances			
Count	3	3	1
Average	43.5%	37.6%	33.8%
Median	42.7%	29.1%	
25th Percentile	36.5%	28.1%	
75th Percentile	50.1%	43.0%	
Sub-Cat. 3 - Drug Delivery			
Count	1	1	3
Average	61.3%	83.5%	44.5%
Median			36.5%
Sub-Cat. 4 - Drug Manufacturers - Major			
Count	12	9	8
Average	30.7%	27.8%	25.8%
Median	28.6%	21.3%	19.5%
25th Percentile	25.7%	20.4%	18.9%
75th Percentile	30.2%	22.2%	20.1%
Sub-Cat. 5 - Drug Manufacturers - Other			
Count	12	10	11
Average	33.6%	25.0%	37.0%
Median	32.8%	24.6%	18.5%
25th Percentile	26.9%	18.8%	16.1%
75th Percentile	39.8%	26.4%	34.5%

Chart XVIII (cont'd)
Healthcare Industry
Costs of Price Protection By Industry Sub-Category

Date of Survey Data	Nov. 2008	Nov. 2009	Dec. 2010
Months To Expiration	26	26	25 1/2
Sub-Cat. 6 - Drug Related Products			
Count	1	2	3
Average	51.6%	35.6%	34.7%
Median			23.0%
Sub-Cat. 7 - Drugs - Generic			
Count	2	2	1
Average	34.4%	21.0%	22.5%
Sub-Cat. 8 - Healthcare Plans			
Count	8	8	5
Average	41.7%	26.3%	19.1%
Median	39.0%	25.9%	19.2%
25th Percentile	37.5%	24.4%	19.2%
75th Percentile	41.1%	28.6%	19.3%
Sub-Cat. 9 - Home Healthcare			
Count	0	1	1
Average		28.1%	33.8%
Sub-Cat. 10 - Hospitals			
Count	0	1	1
Average		36.7%	32.7%
Sub-Cat. 12 - Medical Appliances & Equipment			
Count	5	6	5
Average	31.2%	20.3%	20.3%
Median	27.0%	18.9%	19.9%
25th Percentile	26.3%	18.7%	19.5%
75th Percentile	38.7%	22.3%	22.2%
Sub-Cat. 13 - Medical Instruments & Supplies			
Count	4	4	4
Average	44.1%	18.9%	19.2%
Median	49.0%	16.9%	17.0%
25th Percentile		16.3%	15.7%
75th Percentile		19.4%	20.4%
Sub-Cat. 14 - Medical Laboratories & Research			
Count	1	2	0
Average	21.5%	19.6%	

Chart XIX
Healthcare Industry
Costs of Price Protection: 2013 Option
(As of December 2010)

		Count	Mean	Median	Range of Mid.-50% *
1	Sub-Cat. 1 - Biotechnology	20	40.5%	36.7%	34.6%
2	Sub-Cat. 2 - Diagnostic Substances	1	33.8%		
3	Sub-Cat. 3 - Drug Delivery	3	44.5%	36.5%	
4	Sub-Cat. 4 - Drug Manufacturers - Major	8	25.8%	19.5%	1.2%
5	Sub-Cat. 5 - Drug Manufacturers - Other	11	37.0%	18.5%	18.4%
6	Sub-Cat. 6 - Drug Related Products	3	34.7%	23.0%	
7	Sub-Cat. 7 - Drugs - Generic	1	22.5%		
8	Sub-Cat. 8 - Healthcare Plans	5	19.1%	19.2%	0.2%
9	Sub-Cat. 9 - Home Healthcare	1	33.8%		
10	Sub-Cat. 10 - Hospitals	1	32.7%		
12	Sub-Cat. 12 - Medical Appliances & Equipment	5	20.3%	19.9%	2.7%
13	Sub-Cat. 13 - Medical Instruments & Supplies	4	19.2%	17.0%	4.7%
15	Sub-Cat. 14 - Medical Laboratories & Research	0			
	Total	63			

* Cost of price protection at the 75th percentile minus cost of price protection at
the 25th percentile.

Thus, it is clear that the more detailed the analysis of LEAPS the more reliable and defensible are the conclusions from their use.

How Fast Do DLOMs Change?

In the four annual studies of LEAPS and the costs of price protection, a major conclusion is that discounts for lack of marketability (DLOMs) are not stable and change dramatically over time. That conclusion raises the obvious question, how often and how fast do discounts change? The answers are: quickly, often and a lot. The factors causing change appear to be conditions in the company, and/or in the industry, and/or in the general economy.

For this study, we chose ten U.S. stocks and recorded the costs of their LEAPS put options on approximately the same dates each month for the first nine months of 2010, beginning on January 19. The ten stocks and their industries were:

Stock Symbol	Company/Business
BP	British Petroleum, PLC Petroleum production and marketing
SLB	Schlumberger Ltd. Petroleum equipment and services

BBY   Best Buy Co.
          Electronics retailer

CAL   Continental Airlines
          International airline

GPS   GAP, Inc.
          Apparel retailer

KBR   KBR, Inc.
          Engineering and construction services

MYGN   Myriad Genetics
          Manufacturers of healthcare diagnostics

RDN   Radian Group
          Surety and title insurer

TCK   Teck Resources Ltd.
          Minerals mining and processing

ZION   Zions Bancorp
          Regional bank holding company

We chose BP to see the effects of the Gulf oil spill on the costs of its LEAPS. We chose SLB (Schlumberger) to see what if any effects the oil spill had on companies related to petroleum producers. For the remaining eight companies, we selected each multiple of 91 companies, alphabetically, from all remaining LEAPS.

We studied only LEAPS expiring on January 21, 2012. In January 2010 those LEAPS had 24 months before expiration. Over the 9-month period from January through September, one would expect some decrease in the cost of price protection (i.e., decrease in the discount percentages) as the holding period (the time to expiration) grew shorter; however, the amount of that decrease can not be identified.

Discount percentages were calculated in the same manner as in all previous studies;[15] that is, by dividing the cost of the put option by the price of the underlying common share on the same day.

The chart on the following page shows the results. As would be expected, the change in cost of price protection on BP stock was dramatic, with a difference between the highest and lowest option costs during the nine month period of 75%. Discounts for Schlumberger (SLB) showed little impact from the BP accident.

Within the nine-month period, it was common for the change in the costs of price protection/discounts to vary from 20% to 30%. In distressed industries or companies (RDN or ZION, for example) the variations could be much greater.

So, what does this mean for appraisers? It simply means that the dates of the data on which you base your DLOM conclusion are important because conditions change fast and often. Your data should be contemporary with your valuation date. In addition, from this and other studies, it is clear that industry and company comparability is important.

---

15 See "Discount Calculations," pg. 10.

LEAPS Costs As % of Stock Prices of
Selected Companies During 9-Month Period of 2010

	BP	SLB	BBY	CAL	GPS	KBR	MYGN	RDN	TCK	ZION
Jan. 19	17.6%	19.2%	18.9%	29.4%	19.5%	23.3%	25.5%	49.1%	23.0%	28.2%
Feb. 17	18.6%	19.2%	18.5%	31.1%	18.8%	23.3%	27.8%	46.7%	24.9%	30.6%
Mar. 17	16.9%	17.7%	16.8%	29.0%	17.2%	20.6%	23.8%	40.4%	20.0%	24.5%
Apr.16	16.3%	17.7%	16.8%	27.1%	15.6%	20.3%	23.1%	37.6%	20.8%	25.1%
May 17	19.7%	21.5%	21.8%	31.1%	19.8%	21.6%	24.8%	41.8%	26.5%	31.9%
June 17	28.5%	20.3%	21.1%	29.0%	18.8%	21.2%	23.6%	41.9%	26.6%	25.9%
July 16	24.1%	20.9%	20.9%	29.3%	19.6%	20.8%	22.5%	39.9%	26.0%	25.0%
Aug. 17	19.5%	19.1%	19.6%	27.5%	18.6%	20.2%	23.4%	39.8%	24.3%	23.2%
Sept. 17	22.4%	17.7%	17.4%	25.3%	17.3%	19.0%	24.9%	34.8%	22.5%	21.3%

Difference: Highest Option Cost ÷ Lowest Option Cost

	BP	SLB	BBY	CAL	GPS	KBR	MYGN	RDN	TCK	ZION
	75.3%	21.6%	29.9%	22.8%	26.8%	22.7%	23.4%	41.2%	32.9%	49.7%

Standard Deviation

	BP	SLB	BBY	CAL	GPS	KBR	MYGN	RDN	TCK	ZION
	3.97	1.42	1.90	1.86	1.39	1.42	1.59	4.37	2.43	3.44

Coefficient of Variation

	BP	SLB	BBY	CAL	GPS	KBR	MYGN	RDN	TCK	ZION
	18.5%	7.4%	10.0%	6.5%	7.6%	6.7%	6.5%	10.6%	10.2%	13.1%

How To Use LEAPS

In general, LEAPS can be used in many of the same ways as the restricted stock studies, and there are 600 to 700 transactions in each. In addition to being industry specific and company specific, LEAPS are valuation date specific; that is they reflect economic conditions on your valuation date, not on some past historical date.

In many valuations we determine a "base" or a "benchmark" from which to increase or decrease the DLOM to arrive at a conclusion. The Tax Court, in its Mandelbaum[16] decision, said "…we use these figures (from 35% to 45%) as benchmarks of the marketability discount for the shares at hand." In the Jelke[17] case, the Court repeatedly used descriptions such as "… (this factor) should also favor a lower-than-average discount." In both cases, the Court had an implicit benchmark although in neither case was that benchmark defined or substantiated. LEAPS can provide a provable benchmark.

---

16 Bernard Mandelbaum, et al. v. Commissioner, T.C. Memo 1995-255, p. 24.
17 Estate of Frazier Jelke, III v. Commissioner, T.C. Memo 2005-131, p.40.

THE ASSIGNMENT

To illustrate how this can be done, let us use an example from an actual appraisal done in 2008, with the facts modified and updated. The client is a small regional stock brokerage company with 2007 revenues of $9,800,000. It has been continuously profitable for many years and has no debt. The company has been in business for over 20 years and has 52 employees of whom 24 are brokers. The interest to be valued is 3.0% of the common stock. There are 32 total shareholders, none of whom has a controlling interest. The subject company is growing at about the same rate as the industry and has paid modest cash distributions. The valuation date is February 15, 2008.

STEP 1: IDENTIFY PUBLIC COMPANIES IN THE INDUSTRY

The first step is to define the industry and obtain a list of public companies in that industry, using SIC or NAICS codes or the website Yahoo Finance. Define the industry as finely as possible. For example, in this assignment we used Yahoo Finance. On the home page (http://finance. yahoo.com), we clicked on the "Investing" tab; then the "Industries" sub-heading; and then the "Complete Industry List." Under the "Financial" sector (one of nine major sectors), we found the "Investment Brokerage – National," and the "Investment Brokerage – Regional" sub-sectors. This search listed 30 companies in "Investment Brokerage – Regional" and 25 companies in "Investment Brokerage – National." While at these sites, it is helpful to download to a spreadsheet the financial data of the companies.[18]

---

18 Be sure to match the financial data to your valuation date. To do so, you may have to obtain earlier years' 10-Ks or 10-Qs from S.E.C.records.

STEP 2: DETERMINE WHICH COMPANIES HAVE LEAPS

This can be done easily by accessing the alphabetical listing of LEAPS at the website of the Chicago Board of Exchange, http://www.cboe. com/TradTool/Symbols/symbolall. aspx. Or, from the CBOE home page, click on "Products," then "LEAPS" from the drop down menu. Under the "LEAPS Resources" paragraph, click on "Equity Options and LEAPS Symbol Directory." For our assignment, there are ten "national" brokerage companies and three "regional" brokerage companies that have LEAPS. On the Yahoo financial spreadsheet you downloaded earlier, delete those companies that do not have LEAPS. The result is shown in the Step 2 chart.

Step 2: Brokerage Firms With LEAPS

Description	Symbol	Market Cap ($)	P/E	ROE %	Div. Yield %	Debt To Equity	Price to Book	Net Profit Margin	Price To Free C.F.
Investm't Brokerage - National		260.34B	29.0	9.4	1.6	12.0	2.4	4.4	-1.4
Investm't Brokerage - Regional		51.16B	23.2	9.8	1.7	0.7	9.1	11.7	-76.7
Charles Schwab Corp.	SHQ	22.07B	9.7	25.6	1.1	0.2	5.9	22.9	NA
E*TRADE Financial Corp.	ETFC	1.73B	NA	41.0	NA	6.9	0.6	NA	NA
Goldman Sachs Group Inc.	GS	63.37B	6.5	29.5	0.9	10.2	1.6	29.9	NA
Lehman Brothers Holdings Inc.	LEH	24.60B	6.4	20.1	1.5	18.2	1.2	20.2	NA
Merrill Lynch & Co., Inc.	MER	43.90B	NA	24.3	3.1	18.2	1.5	NA	NA
Morgan Stanley	MS	44.03B	13.4	7.7	2.7	16.8	1.4	NA	NA
optionsXpress Holdings, Inc.	OXPS	1.31B	13.4	42.6	1.5	NA	4.7	40.7	NA
SEI Investments Co.	SEIC	4.69B	18.8	37.5	0.6	0.1	6.2	15.2	39.1
TD AMERITRADE Corp.	AMTD	10.03B	13.8	35.8	0.0	0.6	4.2	39.1	NA
The Bear Stearns Companies	BSC	9.54B	46.0	1.9	1.8	19.5	0.8	NA	NA
Friedman Billings Ramsey	FBR	288.6M	NA	84.4	10.2	5.4	0.7	NA	NA
Knight Capital Group Inc.	NITE	1.54B	13.4	13.4	NA	0.1	1.7	19.3	NA
Legg Mason Inc.	LM	8.52B	13.1	10.4	1.5	0.2	1.2	13.0	-21.5

Go to the website of the company, Market Data Express, http://www. marketdataexpress.com. Market Data Express provides historical options data for each day on which the stock exchanges are open. They claim that options data is available for the past 16 years. You will have to create an account. On the home page, click on "Search Data." On the "Search Page, Step 1," select "Equities." Then, order by stock symbol and trading date. The cost (as of June 2011) is $3.00 per stock symbol. [19] You will receive a printout like the one in the Step 3 chart (below) showing all options available for each symbol on your valuation date. The LEAPS options information you will need is highlighted in the chart. You can get a chart that interprets the column-heading abbreviations at the Market Data Express website, "Bulk Data" tab, in the second paragraph where it says, "For product information and sample of Optsum click here."

---

19 For $3.00, you may order as many days of data as you wish. I suggest you order data for a couple of days on either side of your valuation date. That way you are sure to avoid non-trading days like weekends or holidays.

Step 3

TRADE_DT	UND_LY	CLS	EXPR_DT	STRK_PRC	PC	OIT	VOL	HIGH	LOW	OPEN	LAST	L_BID	L_ASK	UNDL_PRC	S_TYPE	P_TYPE
20080215	NITE	OTI	20090117	10	C	420	0	0	0	0	0	7.5	7.9	16.88	Leap	Equity
20080215	NITE	OTI	20090117	10	P	86	0	0	0	0	0	0.5	0.65	16.88	Leap	Equity
20080215	NITE	OTI	20090117	12.5	C	479	0	0	0	0	0	5.6	5.9	16.88	Leap	Equity
20080215	NITE	OTI	20090117	12.5	P	253	0	0	0	0	0	1.1	1.25	16.88	Leap	Equity
20080215	NITE	OTI	20090117	15	C	350	0	0	0	0	0	4	4.3	16.88	Leap	Equity
20080215	NITE	OTI	20090117	15	P	435	0	0	0	0	0	1.9	2.05	16.88	Leap	Equity
20080215	NITE	OTI	20090117	17.5	C	5877	0	0	0	0	0	2.7	2.95	16.88	Leap	Equity
20080215	NITE	OTI	20090117	17.5	P	398	0	0	0	0	0	3	3.2	16.88	Leap	Equity
20080215	NITE	OTI	20090117	20	C	1689	0	0	0	0	0	1.7	1.95	16.88	Leap	Equity
20080215	NITE	OTI	20090117	20	P	87	0	0	0	0	0	4.5	4.7	16.88	Leap	Equity
20080215	NITE	OTI	20090117	22.5	C	419	0	0	0	0	0	1	1.15	16.88	Leap	Equity
20080215	NITE	OTI	20090117	22.5	P	30	0	0	0	0	0	6.2	6.5	16.88	Leap	Equity
20080215	NITE	OTI	20090117	25	C	402	0	0	0	0	0	0.55	0.75	16.88	Leap	Equity
20080215	NITE	OTI	20090117	25	P	0	0	0	0	0	0	8.3	8.6	16.88	Leap	Equity
20080215	NITE	OTI	20090117	30	C	61	0	0	0	0	0	0.1	0.25	16.88	Leap	Equity
20080215	NITE	YTI	20100116	10	P	125	0	0	0	0	0	0.9	1.35	16.88	Leap	Equity
20080215	NITE	YTI	20100116	12.5	C	18	0	0	0	0	0	6.1	7	16.88	Leap	Equity
20080215	NITE	YTI	20100116	12.5	P	16	0	0	0	0	0	1.55	2.05	16.88	Leap	Equity
20080215	NITE	YTI	20100116	15	C	106	0	0	0	0	0	5	5.5	16.88	Leap	Equity
20080215	NITE	YTI	20100116	15	P	219	0	0	0	0	0	2.45	3	16.88	Leap	Equity
20080215	NITE	YTI	20100116	17.5	C	33	0	0	0	0	0	3.5	4.2	16.88	Leap	Equity
20080215	NITE	YTI	20100116	17.5	P	34	0	0	0	0	0	3.6	4.4	16.88	Leap	Equity
20080215	NITE	YTI	20100116	20	C	65	0	0	0	0	0	2.65	3.4	16.88	Leap	Equity
20080215	NITE	YTI	20100116	20	P	0	0	0	0	0	0	5.2	6	16.88	Leap	Equity
20080215	NITE	YTI	20100116	22.5	C	111	0	0	0	0	0	1.85	2.6	16.88	Leap	Equity
20080215	NITE	YTI	20100116	22.5	P	20	0	0	0	0	0	6.9	7.7	16.88	Leap	Equity
20080215	NITE	YTI	20100116	25	C	45	0	0	0	0	0	1.5	2	16.88	Leap	Equity
20080215	NITE	YTI	20100116	25	P	0	0	0	0	0	0	8.7	9.6	16.88	Leap	Equity

Step 4: Calculate Costs of Price Protection On Your Valuation Date

Using the options information from Market Data Express, calculate the cost of a put option as a percentage of the stock price on the valuation date. In our studies of LEAPS, we adjust the option cost if it is more than 1% different from the stock price. We call this a "Distance Weighted Option Cost." It is simply the relationship between the actual stock price and the next higher and lower option strike prices. For example, using the information shown in the Step 3 chart, we will calculate the discount or cost of price protection for the Knight Capital LEAPS (symbol NITE) shown in the Step 4 chart – for the longer term LEAPS expiring on January 16, 2010, about 23 months in the future. The Step 3 chart shows that NITE has a put option available at a "strike price" of $15.00 per share for $3.00 ("L_ASK" or "Last Asked" price) and another at a strike price of $17.50 for $4.40 per share. The Step 3 chart also shows that the closing price of NITE stock on February 15, 2008 was $16.88 per share (the column headed "UNDL_PRC"). The stock price is $1.88 above the $15.00 strike price, or 75.2% of the $2.50 difference in strike prices ($1.88 ÷ $2.50). The difference in put option costs is $1.40 ($4.40 - $3.00). So we add 75.2% of the difference ($1.40 x .752 = $1.05) to the lower option cost ($3.00) to arrive at a "Distance Weighted Option Cost" of $4.05 ($3.00 + $1.05). Dividing that by the stock price results in a percentage cost of price protection of 24.0% ($4.05 ÷ $16.88).

The Step 4 chart shows the discounts on February 15, 2008 for the thirteen brokerage companies that have LEAPS. The expiration date of the 2010 LEAPS, January 16, is about 23 months after our valuation date, February 15, 2008. The January 17 expiration date for 2009

LEAPS is 11 months after our valuation date. Some general observations can be drawn from this data. The cost of LEAPS for even the largest companies in the industry like Goldman Sachs, Morgan Stanley and Merrill Lynch is 20% or more. The cost at the 75th percentile is 25%.

Step 4: Public Brokerage Companies With LEAPS
Cost of Price Protection, as of Feb. 15, 2008

Company	Symbol	Stock Price	Jan. '09 LEAPS				Jan. '10 LEAPS			
			Strike Price	Option Cost	Dist. Wghtd. Cost	Disct.	Strike Price	Option Cost	Dist. Wghtd. Cost	Disct.
Charles Schwab	SCHW	$20.05	$20.00	$3.00	N.A.	15.0%	$20.00	$4.20	N.A.	20.9%
E*TRADE Financial	ETFC	$5.13	$5.00	$1.65			$5.00	$2.20		
			$7.50	$3.40	1.74	33.9%	$7.50	$4.00	$2.29	44.6%
Goldman Sachs	GS	$175.54	$175.00	$25.60	N.A.	14.6%	$170.00	$32.10		
							$180.00	$37.10	$34.87	19.9%
Lehman Brothers	LEH	$54.10	$50.00	$8.10			$50.00	$11.20		
			$55.00	$10.40	9.99	18.5%	$60.00	$16.30	$13.29	24.6%
Merrill Lynch	MER	$50.90	$50.00	$8.40			$50.00	$11.40		
			$55.00	$11.00	8.87	17.4%	$55.00	$14.10	$11.89	23.4%
Morgan Stanley	MS	$42.36	$40.00	$6.00			$40.00	$8.20		
			$45.00	$8.50	7.18	16.9%	$45.00	$10.80	$9.42	22.2%
optionsXpress	OXPS	$25.31	$25.00	$3.90			$25.00	$5.20		
			$27.50	$5.40	4.08	16.1%	$27.50	$8.50	$5.36	21.2%
SEI Investments	SEIC	$25.35	$25.00	$3.50			$25.00	$6.90		
			$30.00	$6.80	3.73	14.7%	$30.00	$9.40	$7.08	27.9%
TD AMERITRADE	AMTD	$18.02	$17.50	$2.25			$15.00	$2.30		
			$20.00	$3.70	2.55	14.2%	$20.00	$4.70	$3.74	20.8%
Bear Stearns	BSC	$82.47	$80.00	$12.90			$80.00	$16.40		
			$85.00	$15.30	14.08	17.1%	$90.00	$20.90	$17.53	21.3%
Friedman Billings	FBR	$2.97	$2.50	$0.75			$2.50	$0.95		
			$5.00	$2.40	1.06	35.7%	$5.00	$2.75	$1.29	43.4%
Knight Capital	NITE	$16.88	$15.00	$2.05			$15.00	$3.00		
			$17.50	$3.20	2.91	17.2%	$17.50	$4.40	$4.05	24.0%
Legg Mason Inc.	LM	$69.04	$60.00	$5.50			$60.00	$8.60		
			$70.00	$9.70	9.28	13.4%	$70.00	$13.00	$12.56	18.2%
		Median				16.9%				22.2%
		25th Percentile				14.7%				20.9%
		75th Percentile				17.4%				24.6%

Step 5: Analyze The Data To Determine A Reasonable Benchmark Discount

You can analyze the data in the same way you would analyze the data for a publicly traded guideline company. One (of several) ways to do so is to use a chart like that shown for Step 5 (below) which utilizes data from the spreadsheet you downloaded from Yahoo Finance. The object of this analysis is to determine a reasonable benchmark range of discounts for your subject company. For example, our research on the entire universe of LEAPS shows that discounts (or costs of price protection) increase significantly as company size decreases or as risk increases. These characteristics are obvious in the 44.6% discount of E*Trade Financial (ETFC) and the 43.4% discount of Friedman Billings Ramsey (FBR), both of which had financial difficulties in 2007. Yet these companies are hundreds of times larger in revenues or assets than the company we are valuing. The three companies whose operations are most similar to our subject's are Schwab (SCHW) at 20.9% discount, TDAmeritrade (AMTD) at 20.8%, and E*Trade at 44.6%. The five companies with 2007 revenues under $2 billion have discounts ranging from 21.2% to 44.6%. Considering the very small size of our subject company, it is hard to imagine anyone arguing for a discount for our subject lower than 25%, the 75th percentile of all 13 companies. This sets an important lower limit for our discount conclusion.

Comparing our subject to the public companies, we can see a strength in that the subject has no debt and has a better than average return on equity for "Investment Brokerage – Regional." However, its profit margin percentage, 4.0%, is before taxes and still is less than half the margin of the public companies (which report after tax profits). Still, the subject does not have financial problems of the magnitude of ETFC or FBR. Consequently, an upper limit for a discount is probably around 40%.

Step 5: Analysis of Public Companies With LEAPS
(Latest fiscal yearends; dollars in millions)

Description	Symbol	Total Revenues	Total Assets	Ratio Revs./Assets	P/E	ROE %	Div. Yield %	Debt to Equity	Price to Book	Net Profit Margin	Ops. (a)
Investm't Brokerage - Natl.					11.5	18.3	1.3	12.0	2.2	8.9	
Investm't Brokerage - Regl.					27.9	7.7	1.3	0.8	9.1	10.8	
Charles Schwab Corp.	SCHW	$4,994.0	$42,286.0	0.12	10.0	26.7	1.0	0.2	6.7	22.9	1
E*TRADE Financial Corp.	ETFC	-$378.0	$56,845.9	N.M.	NA	-41.0	NA	6.9	0.8	NA	1
Goldman Sachs Group	GS	$45,987.0	$691,063.0		7.6	29.5	0.7	10.2	1.8	29.9	3
Lehaman Brothers	LEH	$19,257.0	$1,020,050	0.03	8.3	20.1	1.1	18.2	1.5	20.2	3
Merrill Lynch	MER	$11,250.0	$1,020,050	0.01	NA	-22.2	2.6	16.6	1.3	NA	3
Morgan Stanley	MS	$28,026.0	$1,045,409	0.03	14.5	7.7	2.4	16.8	1.5	NA	3
optionsXpress	OXPS	$247.0	$1,155.5	0.21	16.2	42.6	1.0	NA	5.7	40.7	2
SEI Investments Co.	SEIC	$1,369.0	$1,252.4	1.09	20.4	37.5	0.5	0.1	6.7	15.2	3
TD AMERITRADE	AMTD	$2,283.4	$18,859.2	0.12	14.6	35.8	0.0	0.6	4.4	39.1	1
Bear Stearns Companies	BSC	$5,945.0	$395,362.0	0.02	53.0	1.9	1.5	19.5	1.0	NA	3
Friedman Billings Ramsey	FBR	$105.5	$2,469.5	0.04	NA	-41.5	5.9	5.8	0.8	NA	3
Knight Capital Group, Inc.	NITE	$669.1	$1,755.8	0.38	13.4	13.4	NA	0.1	1.7	19.3	3
Legg Mason, Inc.	LM	$4,343.7	$9,604.5	0.45	14.6	NA	1.3	0.1	1.4	13.0	2
Subject Company		$9.8 *	$4.4	2.23		11.7		0.0		4.0 (b)	

(a) "Operations" - Similarity of operations to subject:
Criterion: Primary business is financial services to individuals.
1 = most similar to subject
2 = some similarities to subject
3 = least similar to subject
(b) Earnings before tax (S-corp.)

71

The argument will be made, of course, that none of these companies is precisely comparable to our subject. Generally that will be true. But, our objective in Step 5 is not to determine an exact discount but to set reasonable, defensible minimum and maximum levels or benchmark discounts. Moreover, these discounts are industry specific, valuation date specific, and are established by the market.

STEP 6: REACH A FINAL DISCOUNT CONCLUSION WITH THE USE OF A MANDELBAUM CONSTRUCT

In arriving at a conclusion, we have found useful the chart on a following page which examines the Mandelbaum case factors and ranks their influence relative to the public companies that have LEAPS. In this regard, it is important to keep in mind the factors that are intrinsic to LEAPS of the public company group such as: a) they are small, non-influential share holdings; b) they already contain industry specific risk; c) they contain company specific risk and volatility expectations; d) they have known holding periods (in this case, 11 months for 2009 LEAPS or 23 months for 2010 LEAPS); and they reflect economic and market conditions on the valuation date. It is also important to remember and apply the results of our annual studies of LEAPS showing the factors that influence DLOMs and the extents of those influences: company size and risk are the most important factors. Profitability, dividend yields, and other financial measures are considerably less important, except in extreme manifestations. Then, you can weigh each factor and determine a discount conclusion for your company's specific characteristics. A Mandelbaum construct also helps to remind us of factors not embedded in any of the LEAPS, such as restrictions on transfers of shares, likely cost of a public offering, an influential-size shareholding, an unusual cash distribution policy, or others.

The Step 6 chart compares our subject company to the industry group of 13 companies that have publicly traded LEAPS. It helps crystallize the factors contributing to a marketability discount conclusion within the range of 25% to 40% that we have determined. Analysis of the five companies that are "most similar" or "somewhat similar" in operations to our subject (Charles Schwab, E*Trade Financial, TD AMERITRADE, optionsXpress, Legg Mason) helps to focus on the strengths and weaknesses of the company we are appraising. First, we ignore E*Trade Financial and its cost of price protection because it has serious financial problems at this time which our subject does not have. Of the remaining four companies, all except Legg Mason have returns on equity more than double those of our company. None has significant debt which is comparable to our company, but all have profit margins three or more times the size of our subject. Their discounts range from a low of 18.2% (Legg Mason) to a high of 21.2% (optionsXpress).

We know from our annual studies of LEAPS that size and risk are primary determinants of the costs of price protection. The Mandelbaum factor of "Financial Statement Analysis" suggests that our subject's low profitability is offset by its long history of profitability. It has no debt. Thus, we judge the financial condition of the company to have a "neutral" affect on our discount conclusion. However, in the "Company/Industry" category we must recognize that the company we are appraising is very small in the industry (with less than $10 million of revenues), operates in a small geographic area, and has a narrow line of products and services. These facts require a significant increase in the discount as compared to the public companies. Other important factors are the subject's lack of management depth, its right of first refusal on transfers, and a redemption price lower than fair market value. The key offsetting factor is a short holding period provided by the Company's redemption policy. Overall it would be reasonable to conclude a discount for lack of marketability of 35% for our subject.

Step 6: Mandelbaum DLOM Factors

Compared To Public Company Peer Group

Factor	Comparison	Affect On DLOM	Weight In Conclusion
Financial Statement Analysis debt/equity ratio; profitability; growth; stability; risk	- Strong balance sheet - Low profitability but long hisory of profitability - Growth comparable to industry	Neutral	20%
Dividend/Distributin Policy size; consistency; growth	- Comparable to industry	None	0%
Company/Industry size; position in industry; history; outlook	- Very small in size. Non-influential. - Small geographic market - No significant products or services other than brokerage.	Increases	40%
Company Management experience; depth	- Experienced management but little depth.	Increases	10%
Amount of Control In Transferred Shares	- None. Comparable to public companies.	None	0%
Restrictions On Transfer	- Company has right of first refusal on transfers to other than current shareholders and their families.	Increases	10%
Anticipated Holding Period	- 1 to 2 years. Comparable to LEAPS.	None	0%
Company Redemption Policy policy; financial capability; history	- Company redeems "small amounts" of shares annually for cash (at Company's discretion). - Redemption price is adjusted book value which is lower than fair market value.	Neutral	20%
Likely Cost of Public Offering legal ability; financial ability to afford cost	- Public offering unlikely. Cost high.	None	0%

It may be tempting to apply a mathematical approach to reach a DLOM conclusion by using one or more results from the LEAPS studies. For instance, since the revenues of our subject are under $100 million, we can apply an adder of 9.1% to our base discount because the LEAPS studies in 2006 showed that the median discount for companies with under $100 million in revenues was 9.1% greater than the median discount for companies with under $1 billion in revenues. There is no rationale for such an approach, and a Mandelbaum-type analysis and weighting of all of the various marketability factors is much more reasonable.

CONCLUSION

Although LEAPS do not provide a DLOM "answer," it is clear that by using them we can prove a base discount (for companies with similar characteristics) and make defensible estimates of upper and lower ranges of discount. In this way, the analysis of LEAPS provides much better substantiation of the discount conclusion.

LEAPS On ETFs
(Exchange Traded Funds)

Several years ago we noticed that a few LEAPS were being traded on ETFs. Since that time, many more LEAPS are available on ETFs, and I expect the numbers will continue to grow. The interest for appraisers of closely-held interests is that we commonly hear that highly diversified portfolios warrant very low, if any, discounts for lack of marketability, and/or that publicly traded stocks in an entity like a family limited partnership also require small discounts. Observation of LEAPS put options on ETFs raises serious questions about those assumptions. In addition, it highlights the differences in risk among various industries and/or investments.

In early December 2010, 86 LEAPS were available to purchase on Exchange Traded Funds.[20] ETFs are similar in makeup to mutual funds and are traded on several exchanges. Generally, ETFs hold stocks or other assets with a common trait, such as stocks in the pharmaceutical industry or the semiconductor industry, a Standard and Poor's index

---

20 Appendix A gives a brief description of selected ETFs for which LEAPS are available in early December 2010.

or a Russell index, gold or petroleum, consumer staples or real estate. ETFs may hold as few as 10 or 15 stocks or 100 or more. The common trait enables an investor to focus in an industry or an asset class and to achieve some diversification at the same time.

In the 2010 study we eliminated two groups of ETFs: a) those centered on foreign companies or foreign traits, such as a fund on the Japanese yen (symbol FXY) and one made up of the stocks of Brazilian companies (symbol EWZ), and b) those centered on exotic financial plays, such as 3X an Emerging Markets Index (symbol EDZ) or 3X a Small Cap Bear Index (symbol TZA).

43 ETFs remained for which 2012 options could be purchased and 35 for which 2013 options were available. To make those groups more relevant, we further divided them into four segments based on their underlying nature:
- – ETFs investing in the stocks of operating companies;
- – ETFs based on various indices, such as the S&P 500 Index;
- – ETFs based on or investing in commodities; and,
- – ETFs based on or investing in bonds.

Chart XX shows the ETFs based on stocks of operating companies. The median discount for the 2013 put options of all 25 companies is 17.6% and the average is 19.3%. The minimum discount is 12.6% for the "Consumer Staples" ETF (symbol XLP) and the maximum discount is 34.8% for the "Homebuilders" ETF (symbol XHB). To some extent, these and other ETFs can be compared to the "Industry" groups defined by Yahoo Finance and described earlier.

Chart XX

Exchange Traded Funds Analysis
ETFs Based on Stocks of Companies

Symbol	Name	2012 Discount	2013 Discount
XLP	CONSUMER STAPLES SECTOR SPDR	9.7%	12.6%
XLE	ENERGY SECTOR SPDR	11.9%	16.7%
XLF	FINANCIAL SECTOR SPDR	12.6%	17.6%
XLI	INDUSTRIAL SECTOR SPDR	11.8%	16.0%
IYR	ISHARES DJ US REAL EST IDX FD	13.7%	20.3%
IYT	ISHARES DOW JONES TRANSP AVG INDEX	13.6%	
IBB	ISHARES NASDAQ BIOTECH INDX FD	10.8%	15.0%
SLV	ISHARES SILVER TRUST	16.0%	21.5%
GDXJ	MKT VECTORS JUNIOR GOLD MINERS	18.7%	26.0%
GDX	MKT VECTORS GOLD MINERS INDEX	16.0%	20.7%
OIH	OIL SERVICES TR	14.6%	20.2%
XOP	SPDR OIL & GAS EXP & PROD ETF	13.5%	22.6%
RTH	RETAIL HOLDRS TRUST (HOLDRS)	10.8%	15.4%
XLB	SPDR FD-MATERIALS	14.8%	17.2%
XLV	SPDR FUND-HEALTH CARE	11.6%	13.5%
XLY	SPDR-CONSUMER DISRETI	11.9%	17.5%
SMH	SEMICONDUCTOR HOLDERS TR	18.5%	18.5%
XME	SPDR S&P METALS & MINING ETF	19.0%	24.8%
DIA	SPDR DOW JONES IND AV ETF TRUST	9.6%	13.8%
GLD	SPDR GOLD TRUST	10.6%	17.0%
KBE	SPDR KBW BANK ETF	22.3%	29.0%
KRE	SPDR KBW REGIONAL BANKING ETF	14.5%	23.1%
XHB	SPDR S&P HOMEBUILDERS ETF	29.5%	34.8%
XRT	SPDR S&P RETAIL ETF	13.0%	18.1%
XLK	TECHNOLOGY SECTOR SPDR	10.5%	14.9%
XLU	UTILITIES SECTOR SPDR	11.1%	15.4%
VWO	VANGUARD EMERGING MARKETS ETF	14.4%	

	2012	2013
Count	27	25
Average	14.3%	19.3%
Median	13.5%	17.6%
Quartile - 25%	11.3%	15.4%
Quartile - 75%	15.4%	21.5%
Maximum	29.5%	34.8%
Minimum	9.6%	12.6%

The significance of these findings for business valuators is in the industry groupings and results. Many of the subject companies in our appraisals fall within these industries. It is hard to imagine how a DLOM conclusion for a small minority interest in a specific company could be smaller than the discount for the industry's ETF on the same date. For example, an appraisal of a small minority interest in a regional bank in early December 2010 would likely warrant a <u>minimum</u> discount for lack of marketability of 23.1%, the discount on the 52 stocks in the KBW Regional Banking ETF (symbol KRE). From our earlier analysis of various industries as defined by Yahoo Finance, we know that specific company risk is important and varies widely within industries. So, a more detailed analysis by individual companies within the industry would provide even greater confidence in the DLOM conclusion.

Charts XXI, XXII and XXIII show discounts for index-based ETFs, commodities-based ETFs and bond-based ETFs, respectively. For instance, the 2013 discount on a highly diversified investment in the Russell 2000 index (Symbol IWM) is 18.3% (Chart XXI). Similarly, a diversified investment in natural gas (Symbol UNG) carries a cost of price protection for 25 1/2 months of 25.3% (Chart XXII), and an investment in 20+ year U.S. Treasury bonds (Symbol TLT) warrants a discount of 17.7% (Chart XXIII).

Chart XXI
Exchange Traded Funds Analysis
ETFs Based on Various Indices

Symbol	Name	2012 Discount	2013 Discount
DJX	DOW JONES INDL. AVERAGE INDEX	11.8%	
OEF	ISHARES ON THE S&P 100 INDEX FUND	14.8%	
IWM	ISHARES RUSSELL 2000 INDEX	13.2%	18.3%
QQQQ	POWERSHARES QQQ TRUST SERIES 1	11.0%	15.3%
OEX	S&P 100 INDEX	13.9%	
SPY	S&P DEPOSITORY RECEIPTS (SPDRS)	10.2%	14.5%
MDY	S&P MIDCAP SPDR (ETF)	11.4%	16.7%
	Count	7	4
	Average	12.3%	16.2%
	Median	11.8%	16.0%
	Maximum	14.8%	18.3%
	Minimum	10.2%	14.5%

Chart XXII
Exchange Traded Funds Analysis
ETFs Based on Commodities

Symbol	Name	2012 Discount	2013 Discount
DBA	POWERSHS DB AGRICULTURE FUND	13.4%	22.8%
DBC	POWERSHS DB COMMODITY INDEX	11.6%	
UNG	UNITED STATES NATURAL GAS FUND	17.8%	25.3%
USO	UNITED STATES OIL FUND	14.5%	19.1%
	Count	4	3
	Average	14.3%	22.4%
	Median	13.9%	22.8%

Chart XXIII
Exchange Traded Funds Analysis
ETFs Based on Bonds

Symbol	Name	2012 Discount	2013 Discount
IEF	ISHARES 7-10 YEAR TREASURY BOND	7.5%	11.1%
TLT	ISHARES 20+ YEAR TREASURY BOND	10.6%	17.7%
JNK	SPDR BARCLAYS HIGH YIELD BD F	17.1%	24.1%
	Count	3	3
	Average	11.7%	17.6%
	Median	10.6%	17.7%

It is clear that even groupings of broadly diversified stocks or the most secure assets like bonds can have significant costs of price protection when held over relatively short time periods like 25 ½ months (the 2013 option).

Advantages and
Disadvantages of LEAPS

A LEAPS approach to determining a DLOM has several major advantages inherent in it.

1.) The cost of a LEAPS put option is determined by the market on a daily basis. LEAPS prices are not the result of a formula.

2.) LEAPS are valuation-date specific. No adjustments need be made to the data to estimate what the market's volatility is or was. Volatility is already included in the market price of the option.

3.) The maximum holding period of a LEAPS put option (its expiration date) is always known and is never less than 13 months for the longer term option.

4.) By definition, the costs of LEAPS put options include investors' evaluations of the financial, market, management and other risks of each public company and of the company's industry. This provides a market-determined benchmark against which to compare your subject company.

5.) A LEAPS approach is easy for judges, juries and attorneys to understand.

A commonly heard objection to the LEAPS approach is that it is just like the comparable companies approach to valuation except there are fewer companies to compare. Generally that comment is true. The LEAPS approach is similar to the comparable companies approach. And, although there are 600 or 700 possible LEAPS to use, sometimes the group of similar companies is small or the public companies are much larger in size than our subject company. One alternative is to increase the LEAPS sample size by broadening the industry group. But, more important, we know that DLOMs change fast and often. That speed of change demands a market-based approach rather than an historical or formulaic approach.

Strengths and weaknesses of the LEAPS approach are put into perspective when one considers alternative methods of arriving at a DLOM:
   a) using a formula of some type; having to justify each and every input to that formula; and then having to rationalize the result to market conditions on the valuation date; or,
   b) choosing "comparable companies" from a data base of several hundred transactions of some kind that have been accumulated over the last ten years, then adjusting them somehow to reality on your valuation date; and
   c) trying to explain in non-appraiser English either a) or b) to your local circuit court judge.

Another objection to the LEAPS approach was made by an IRS employee who wrote that the LEAPS put option result was too high a discount because any investor could offset the cost by selling a call option on the stock. Theoretically, that is true, but it is unrealistic. When you sell a LEAPS call option, you sell someone else the right to buy your stock, during the next two years, at the same price you paid for it. You earn revenue from the sale, but you have eliminated your opportunity for gain. (If the stock goes up in value during the next two years, the owner of the call option will exercise the option, sell the stock, and take the gain.) Personally, I have never met an investor in a private company who is willing to put a cap on the upside potential of his investment. An investor wants to limit his chance of loss (his downside risk) and leave his chance of gain open. This is precisely what LEAPS put options do.

Appendix A
Selected ETFs With LEAPS
(as of early December 2010)

Symbol	Name	Fund Nature
XLP	CONSUMER STAPLES SECTOR SPDR	Consumer Staples Select Sector Index. 41 co.'s selling food, household products, beverages, etc. Mainly U.S. companies incldg. P&G, Philip Morris, Walmart, Coca-Cola, Kraft.
XLE	ENERGY SECTOR SPDR	Stocks of the Energy Select Sector Index. 41 gas and oil co.'s incldg. Exxon, Chevron, Schlumberger, Apache, etc.
XLF	FINANCIAL SECTOR SPDR	83 stocks of the Financial Select Sector Index, incldg. banks, insurance, finl. services. J.P. Morgan, Wells Fargo, Berkshire Hathaway, etc.
XLI	INDUSTRIAL SECTOR SPDR	59 stocks of the Industrial Select Sector Index, aerospace, machinery, rail, etc. companies, incldg. United Tech., G.E., Caterpillar.
TLT	ISHARES 20+ YEAR TREASURY BOND	Tracks results of Barclays Capital U.S. 20+ Year Treasury Bond Index.
IEF	ISHARES 7-10 YEAR TREASURY BOND	Tracks results of Barclays Capital U.S. 7 - 10 Year Treasury Bond Index.
IYR	ISHARES DJ US REAL EST IDX FD	Tracks results of Dow-Jones U.S. Real Estate Index; 83 stocks, incldg. REITs, R/E holding co.'s. Simon Property, Vornado, Public Storage, etc.
IYT	ISHARES DJ TRANSP AVG INDEX	Holds stocks of 21 companies in D-J Transportation Average; airlines, railroads, trucking, etc. Union Pacific, FedEx, CSX, UPS.
IBB	ISHARES NASDAQ BIOTECH INDX FD	Invests in 123 co.'s in NASDAQ Biotech. Index, such as Amgen Celgene, TEVA, Alexion, etc.
OEF	ISHARES ON THE S&P 100 INDEX FUND	Invests in co.'s in S & P 100 Index - large cap.
IWM	ISHARES RUSSELL 2000 INDEX	Invests in co.'s in Russell 2000 Index
SLV	ISHARES SILVER TRUST	Reflects price of silver owned by the Trust.
GDXJ	MKT VECTORS JUNIOR GOLD MINERS	Stocks of small & medium size, U.S. and foreign co.'s involved primarily in mining for gold or silver.
GDX	MKT VECTORS GOLD MINERS INDEX	Invests in co.'s in NYSE Arca Goldminers Index.

Appendix A (cont'd)
Selected ETFs With LEAPS
(as of early December 2010)

OIH	OIL SERVICES TR	Invests in 18 co.'s in oil services industry, incldg. Schlumberger, Baker Hughes, Halliburton, etc.
XOP	SPDR OIL & GAS EXP & PROD ETF	Invests in 72 co.'s of S&P Oil and Gas Exploration & Production Industry Index. Ex: Petrohawk Energy, Cabot Oil, Bill Barrett Corp.
DBA	POWERSHARES DB AGRICULTURE FUND	Invests in futures contracts on agricultural commodities
DBC	POWERSHARES DB COMMODITY INDEX	Invests in futures contracts on a wide range of commodities, metals, agricultural, plus.
QQQ	POWERSHARES QQQ TRUST SERIES 1	Tracks NASDAQ 100 Index.
RTH	RETAIL HOLDRS TRUST (HOLDRS)	Stock of 20 companies in the Retail Industry.
OEX	S&P 100 INDEX	Tracks S&P 100 Index (not stocks)
SPY	S&P DEPOSITORY RECEIPTS (SPDRS)	All stocks in S&P 500 Index.
MDY	S&P MIDCAP SPDR (ETF)	All stocks in S&P MidCap 400 Index.
XLB	SPDR FD-MATERIALS	Tracks Materials Select Sector Index. 30 co.'s. incldg. chemicals, paper, mining, etc. Examples: DuPont, Dow, Newmont Mining, Alcoa.
XLV	SPDR FUND-HEALTH CARE	Tracks 52 co.'s in Healthcare Select Sector Index. Incldg. biotech, eqpt. & supplies, providers & services Pfizer, J&J, Merck, Amgen, etc.
XLY	SPDR-CONSUMER DISCRETI	79 Co.'s in Consumer Discret.Sector Index. Includes retail, restaurants, autos, household goods, etc. Disney, McDonalds, Comcast, Amazon, Home Depot.
SMH	SEMICONDUCTOR HOLDERS TR	Stocks of 20 co.'s in semiconductor industry. Includes Intel, Applied Matls., Texas Instruments, etc.
XME	SPDR S&P METALS & MINING ETF	45 co.'s in S&P Metals & Mining Industry Index. Ex.: Intl. Coal, RTI Metals, Royal Gold, Carpenter Technol.
JNK	SPDR BARCLAYS HIGH YIELD BD F	Tracks Barclays High Yield Very Liquid Index.
DIA	SPDR DOW JONES IND AV ETF TRUST	Tracks stocks in the DJ Industrial Average Index.
GLD	SPDR GOLD TRUST	Holds gold.

Appendix A (cont'd)
Selected ETFs With LEAPS
(as of early December 2010)

KBE   SPDR KBW BANK ETF   Invests in 26 stocks of KBW Bank Index. JPMorgan,
                                              Citi, Wells Fargo, US Bancorp, etc.

KRE   SPDR KBW REGIONAL BANKING ETF   Invests in 52 stocks of KBW Regional Bank Index.Ex.:
                                              Svb Finl. Grp, Whitney Holdings, Assoc. Banc Corp.

XHB   SPDR S&P HOMEBUILDERS ETF   Invests in 37 stocks of S&P Homebldrs. Industry Index.
                                              Ex.: Aarons; Sher.-Williams; KB Home

XRT   SPDR S&P RETAIL ETF   Invests in 94 stocks of S&P Retail Industry Index. Ex.:
                                              Barnes & Noble, Gamestop, Dillards, NetFlix, Limited

XLK   TECHNOLOGY SECTOR SPDR   Invests in 84 stocks of Technology Sector Index.
                                              Includes computers, software, semicond., etc. Ex.:
                                              Apple, IBM, Microsoft, Google, etc.

UNG   UNITED STATES NATURAL GAS FUND   Invests on futures contracts in natural gas.

USO   UNITED STATES OIL FUND   Invests on futures contracts on crude oil.

XLU   UTILITIES SECTOR SPDR   Invests in 33 stocks of Utilities Sector Index. Includes
                                              utilities of all types. Southern, Exelon, Dominion
                                              Resources, Duke Energy, etc.

VWO   VANGUARD EMERGING MARKETS ETF   Invests in 748 stocks of MSCI Emerging Markets
                                              Index.

Author CV

Statement of
Qualifications   RONALD M. SEAMAN

Professional   FASA (Fellow, American Society of Appraisers)
Qualifications   Accredited in Business Valuation. Recertified 2009.
                     Qualified as an expert witness: Hillsborough, Polk and
                     Pinellas County Circuit Courts; U. S. Bankruptcy Court;
                     U. S. District Court; U. S. Tax Court.
                     Past International President, American Society of Appraisers
                     (2009)
                     Former member (6 years), Business Valuation Committee,
                     American Society of Appraisers.
                     Seminar leader and author.

Business   2006 To Present
Experience   President, DLOM, Inc.   Tampa, FL

                     1985 To Present
                     Founder and Vice President
                     Southland Business Group, Inc.   Tampa, FL

                     Rozier Machinery Co.   Tampa, FL
                     General Manager, Lift Truck Division

                     Champion Products, Inc.   Rochester, NY
                     V. P., Sales and Marketing

Education   M.B.A., Harvard University, Cambridge, MA
                     B.A., Hamilton College, Clinton, NY

Ronald M. Seaman, FASA   DLOM. Inc
Phone: (813) 353-0711   3300 Henderson Blvd., Suite 206A
ronseaman@dlom-info.com   Tampa, Florida 33609